EASY PIANO

BRUNO MARS
UNORTHODOX JUKEBOX

- 2 YOUNG GIRLS
- 9 LOCKED OUT OF HEAVEN
- 16 GORILLA
- 22 TREASURE
- 26 MOONSHINE
- 34 WHEN I WAS YOUR MAN
- 39 NATALIE
- 48 SHOW ME
- 55 MONEY MAKE HER SMILE
- 61 IF I KNEW

ISBN 978-1-4803-3397-0

7777 W. BLUEMOUND RD. P.O. BOX 13819 MILWAUKEE, WI 53213

In Australia Contact:
Hal Leonard Australia Pty. Ltd.
4 Lentara Court
Cheltenham, Victoria, 3192 Australia
Email: ausadmin@halleonard.com.au

For all works contained herein:
Unauthorized copying, arranging, adapting, recording, Internet posting, public performance,
or other distribution of the printed music in this publication is an infringement of copyright.
Infringers are liable under the law.

Visit Hal Leonard Online at
www.halleonard.com

YOUNG GIRLS

Words and Music by BRUNO MARS,
ARI LEVINE, PHILIP LAWRENCE,
JEFF BHASKER and EMILE HAYNIE

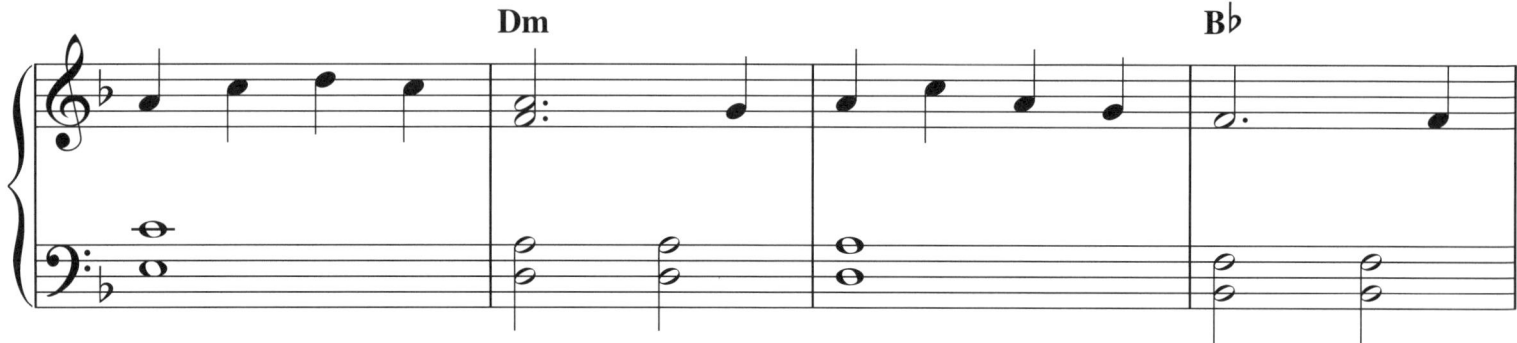

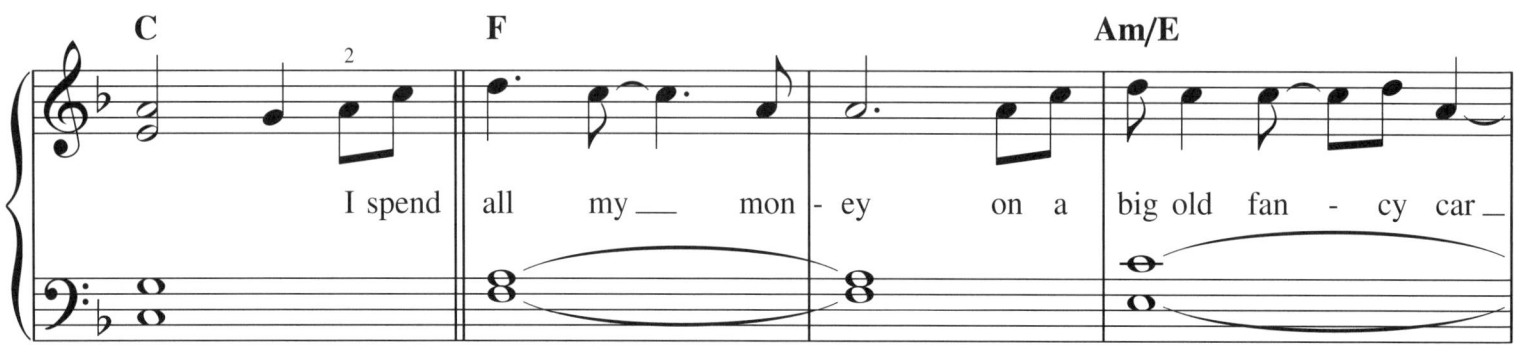

I spend all my money on a big old fancy car for these bright-eyed honeys. Oh yeah, you know who you are.

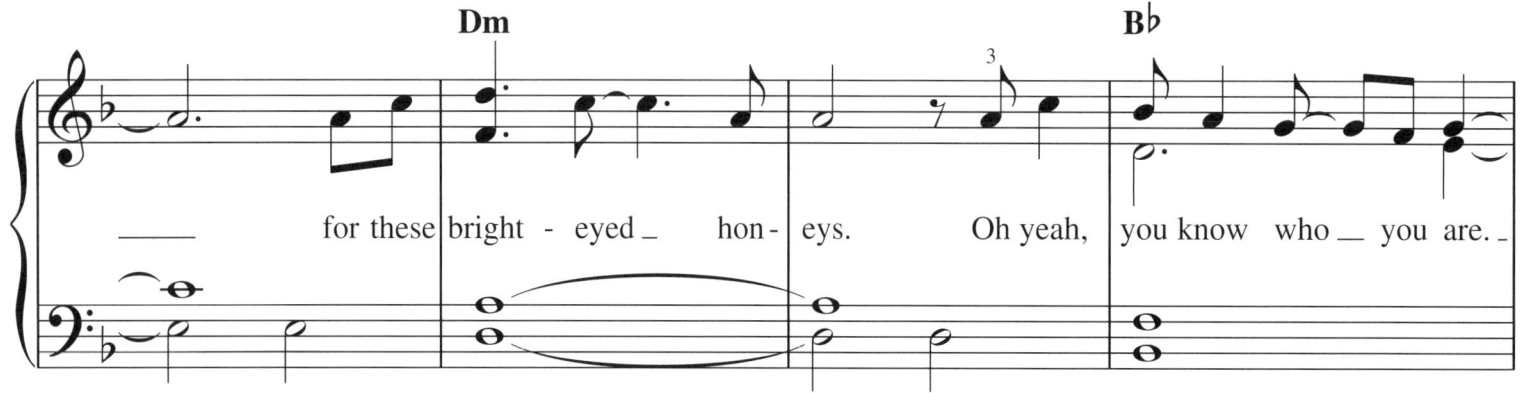

© 2012 BMG GOLD SONGS, MARS FORCE MUSIC, UNIVERSAL MUSIC CORP., TOY PLANE MUSIC, NORTHSIDE INDEPENDENT MUSIC PUBLISHING LLC,
THOU ART THE HUNGER, WB MUSIC CORP., ROC NATION MUSIC, MUSIC FAMAMANEM, SONY/ATV MUSIC PUBLISHING LLC, WAY ABOVE MUSIC and HEAVYCRATE PUBLISHING
All Rights for BMG GOLD SONGS and MARS FORCE MUSIC Administered by BMG RIGHTS MANAGEMENT (US) LLC
All Rights for TOY PLANE MUSIC and HEAVYCRATE PUBLISHING Controlled and Administered by UNIVERSAL MUSIC CORP.
All Rights for THOU ART THE HUNGER Administered by NORTHSIDE INDEPENDENT MUSIC PUBLISHING LLC
All Rights for ROC NATION MUSIC and MUSIC FAMAMANEM Administered by WB MUSIC CORP.
All Rights for SONY/ATV MUSIC PUBLISHING LLC and WAY ABOVE MUSIC Administered by SONY/ATV MUSIC PUBLISHING LLC, 8 Music Square West, Nashville, TN 37203
All Rights Reserved   Used by Permission

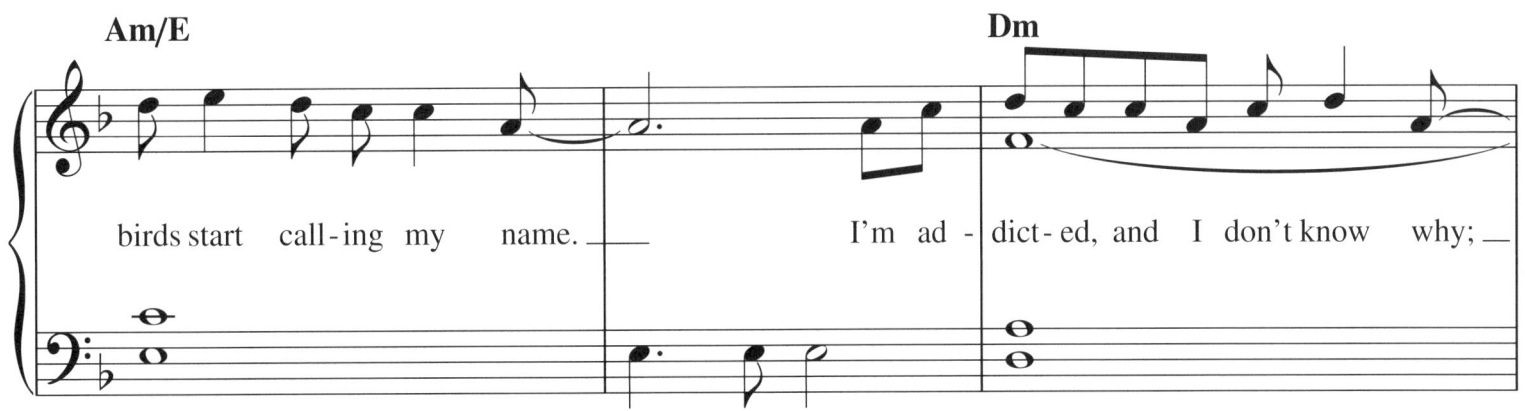

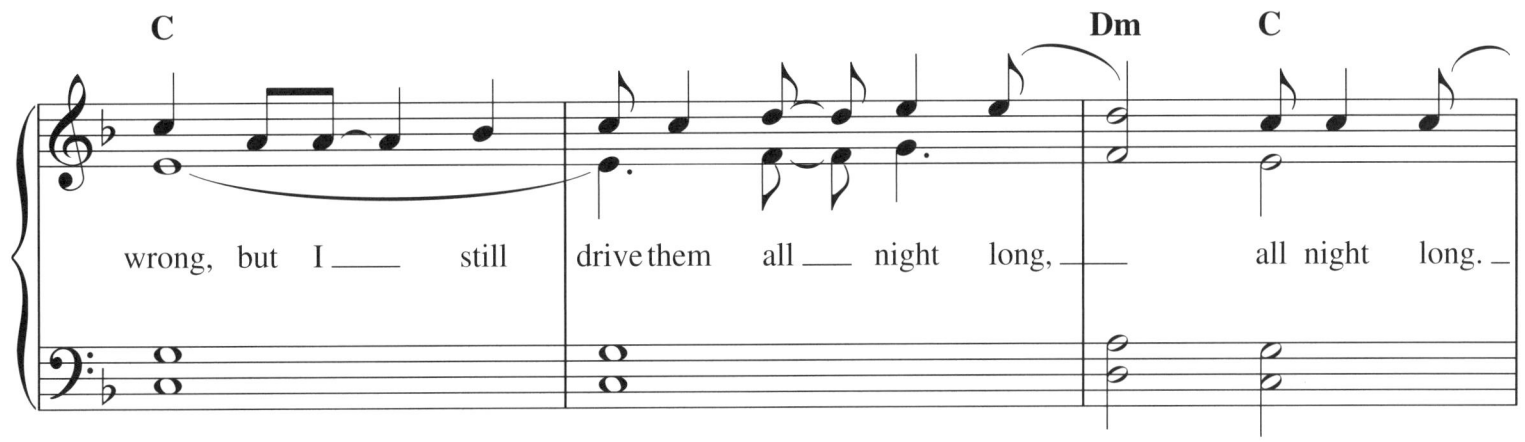

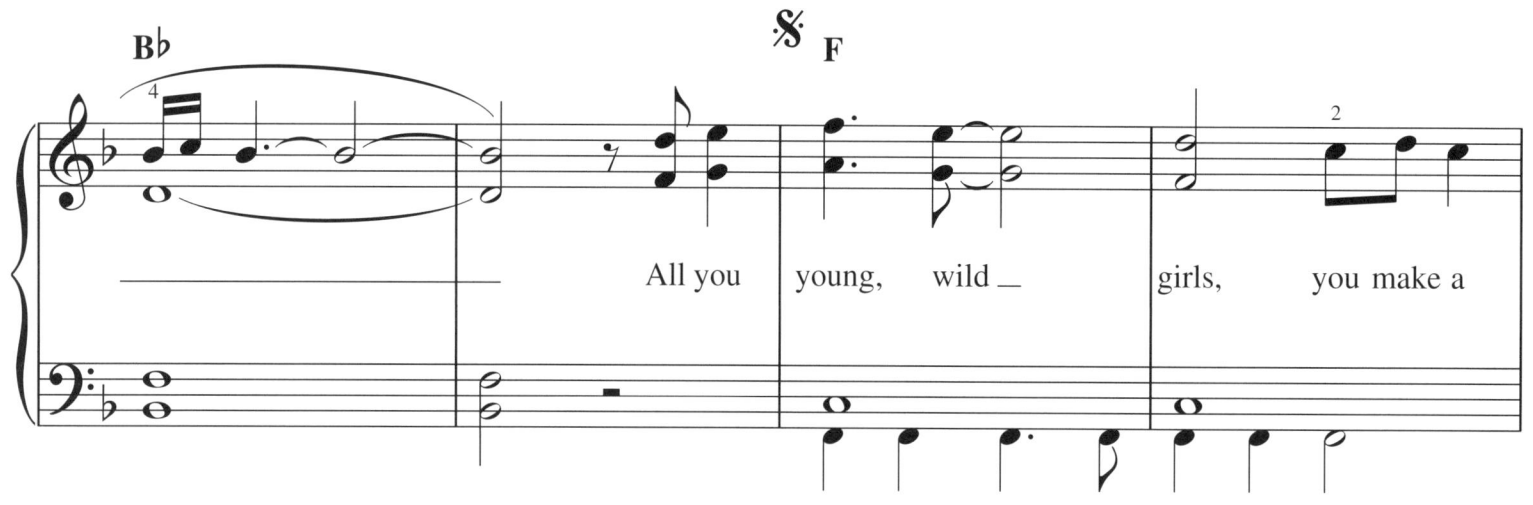

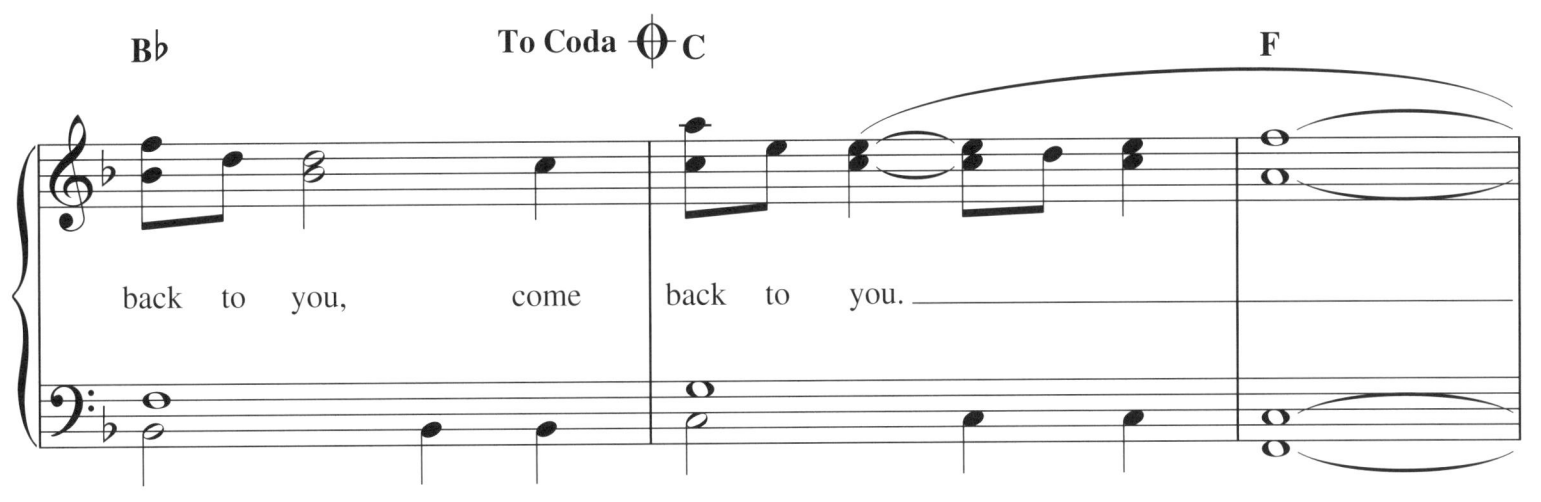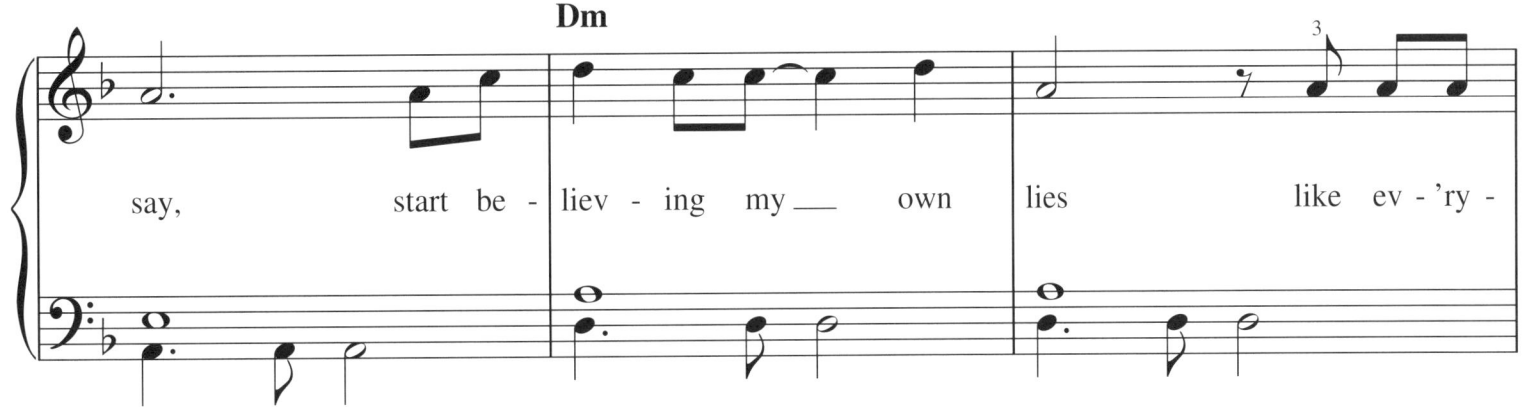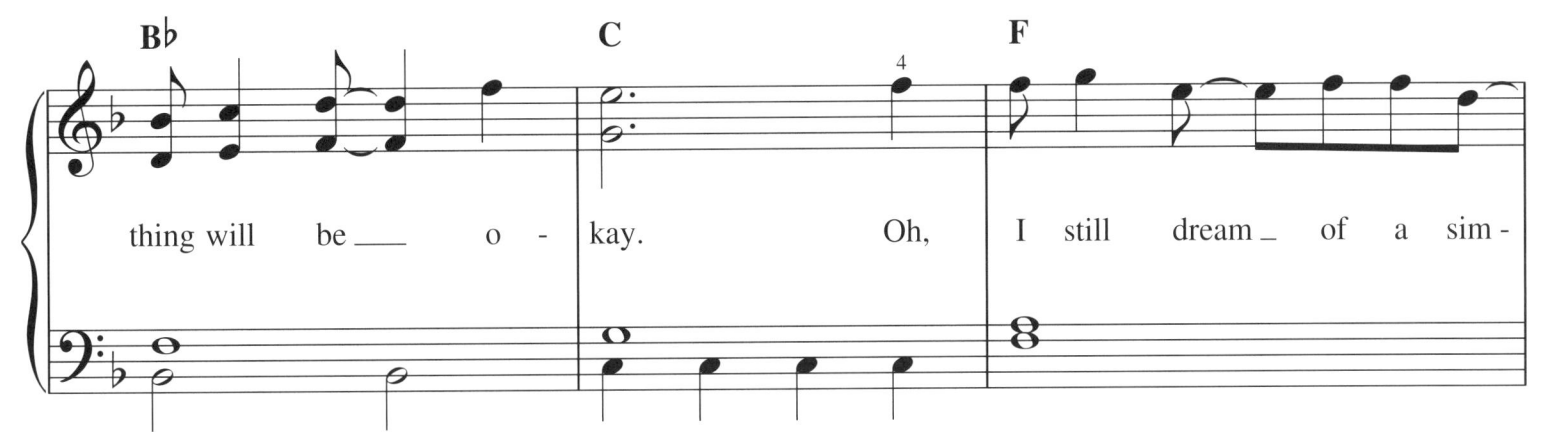

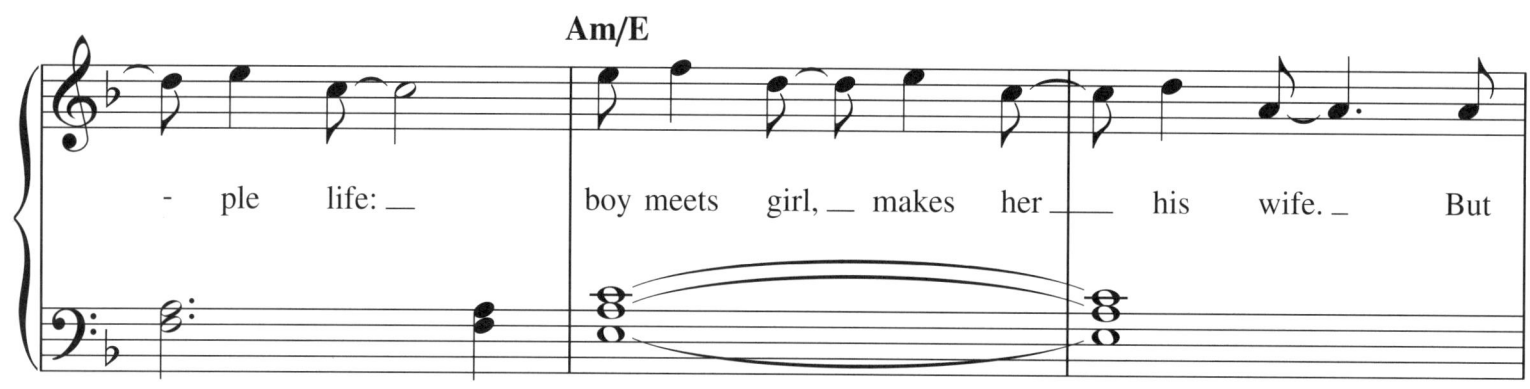

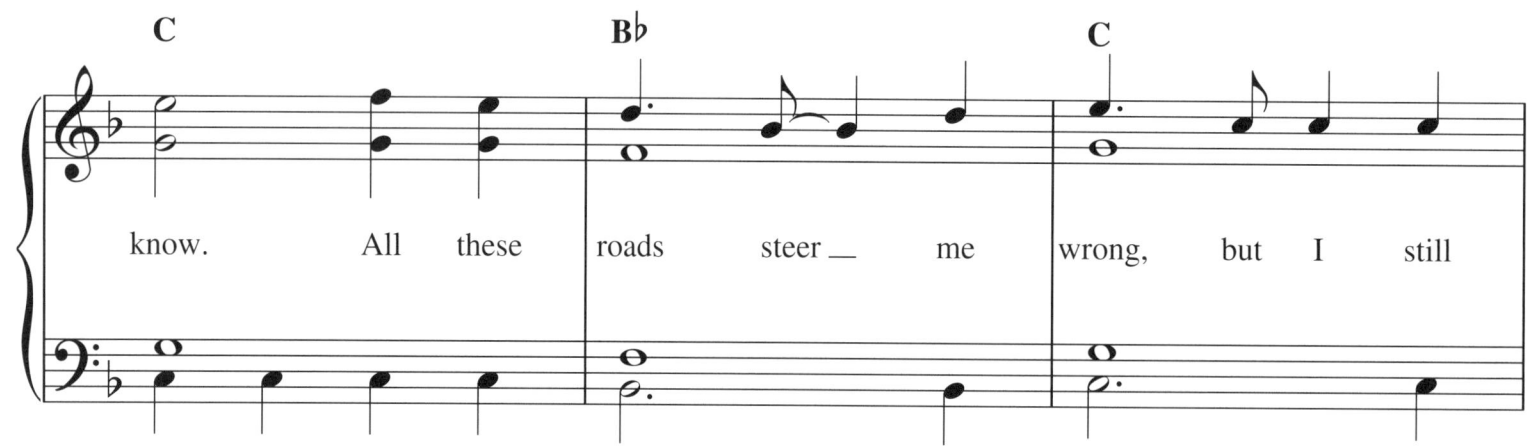
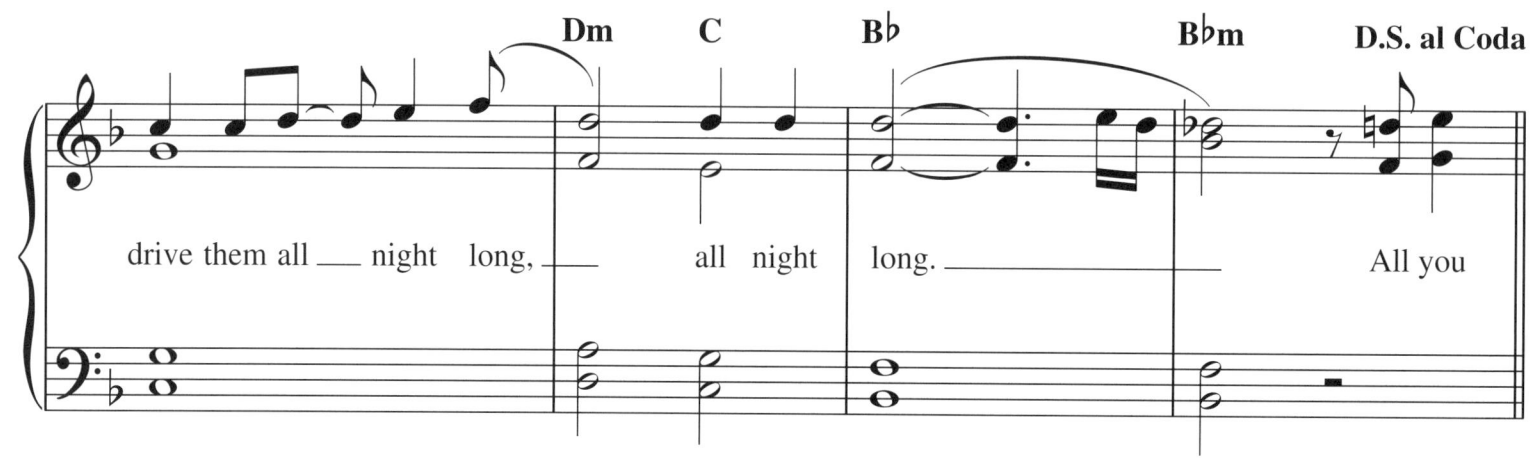

Am/C
A/C♯
Dm
B♭
Yeah, you young, wild _ girls, you'll be the death of me, the
C
F
Am
death of me. All you young, wild _ girls, no mat - ter what you do,
Dm
yeah, you young, wild _ girls, I al - ways come
B♭
C
F
back to you, come back to you. ___
rit.

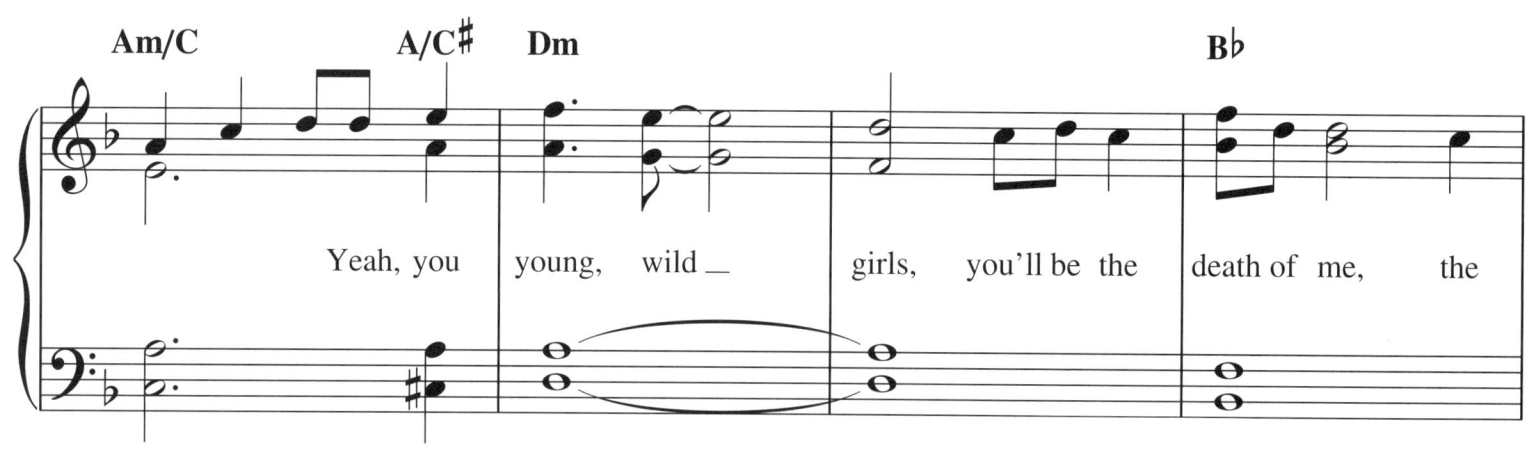

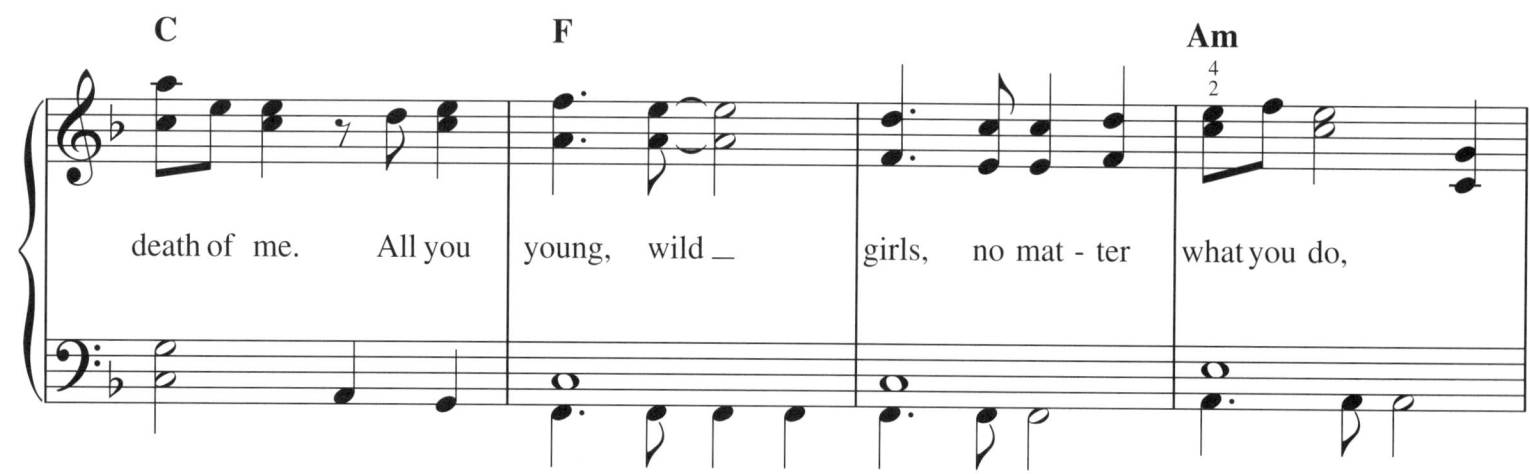

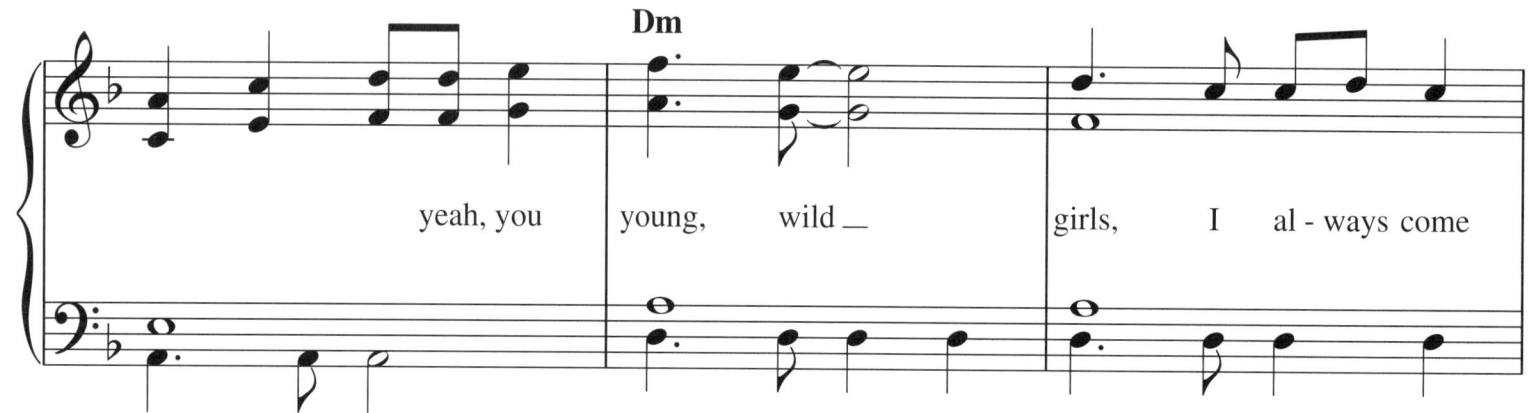

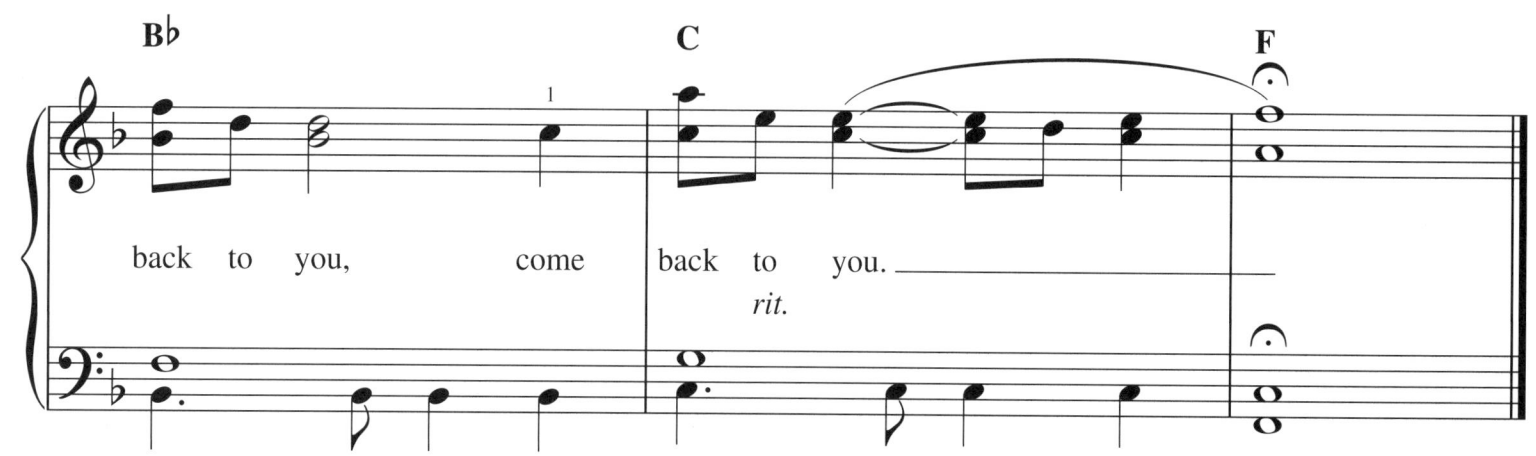

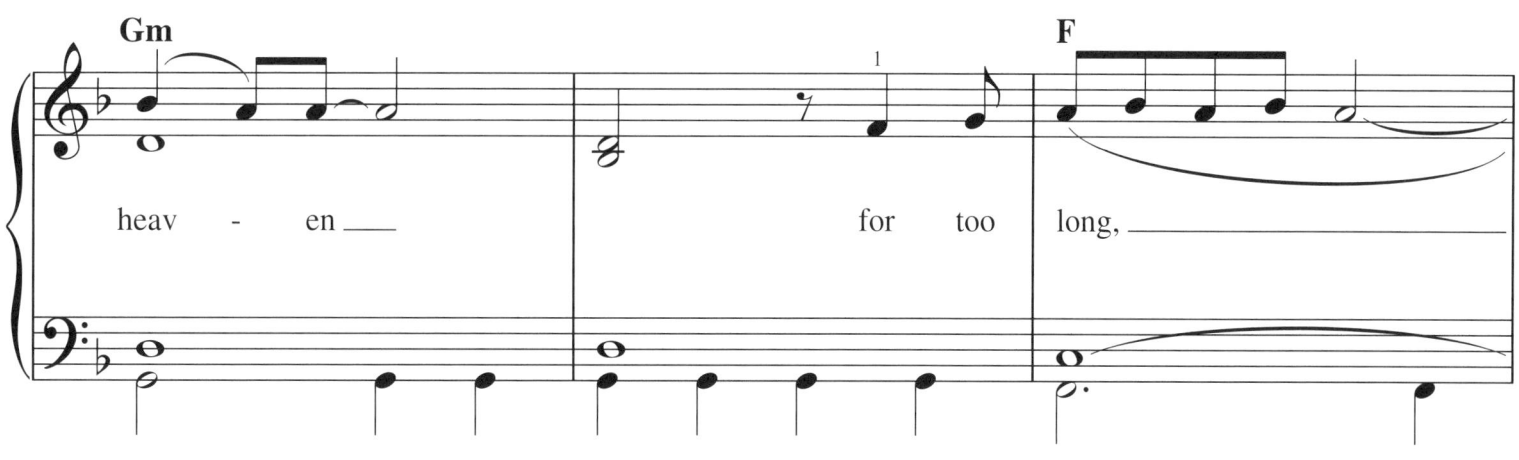
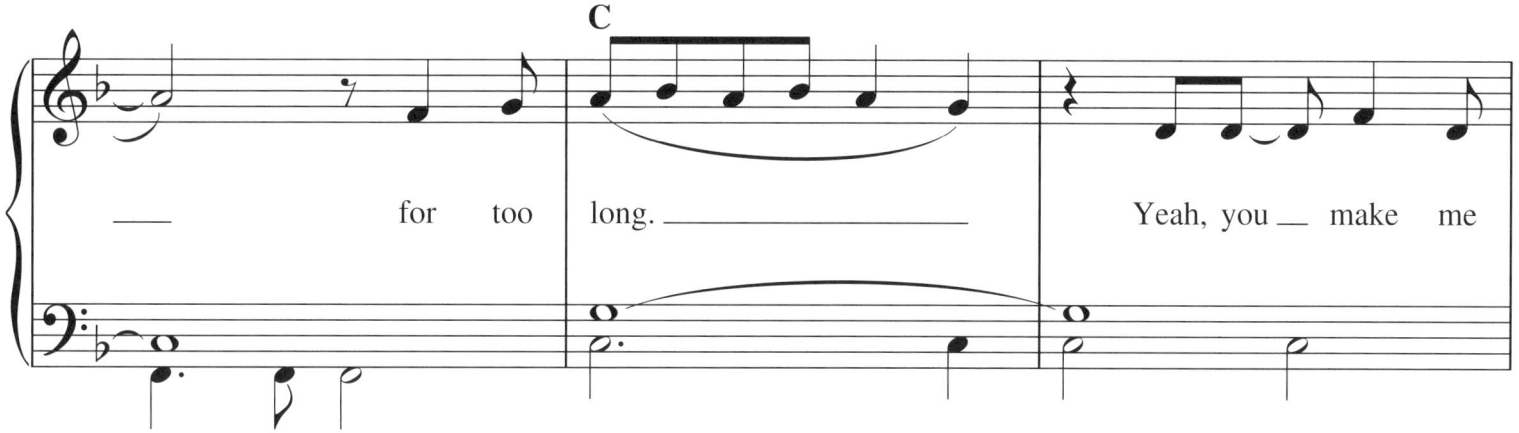

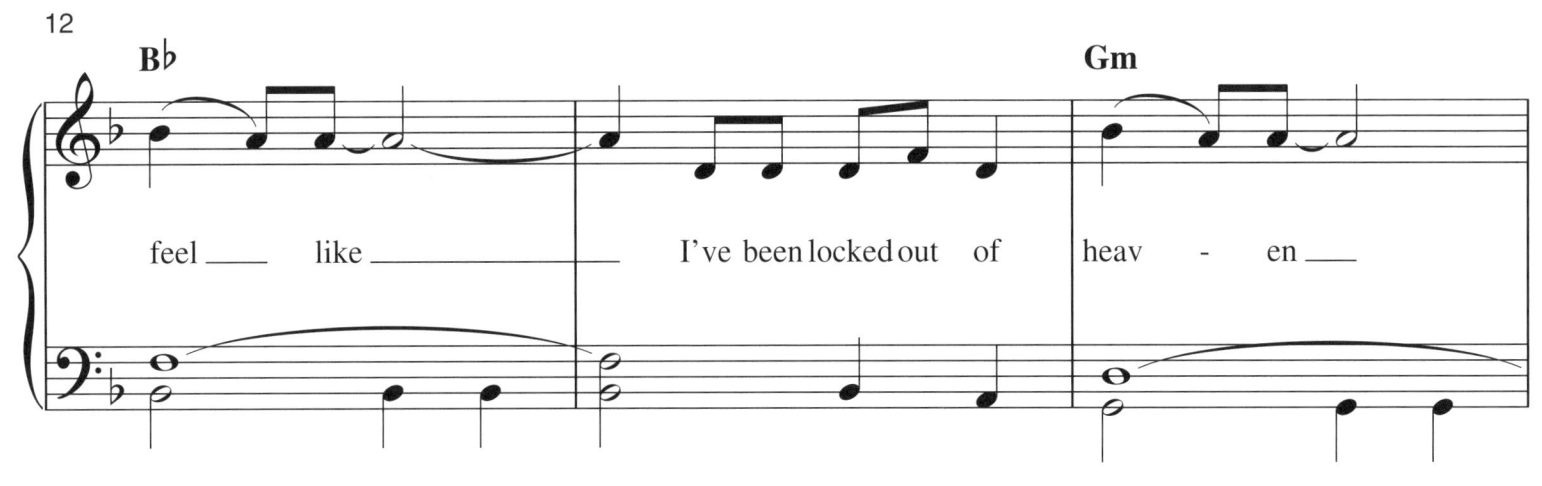
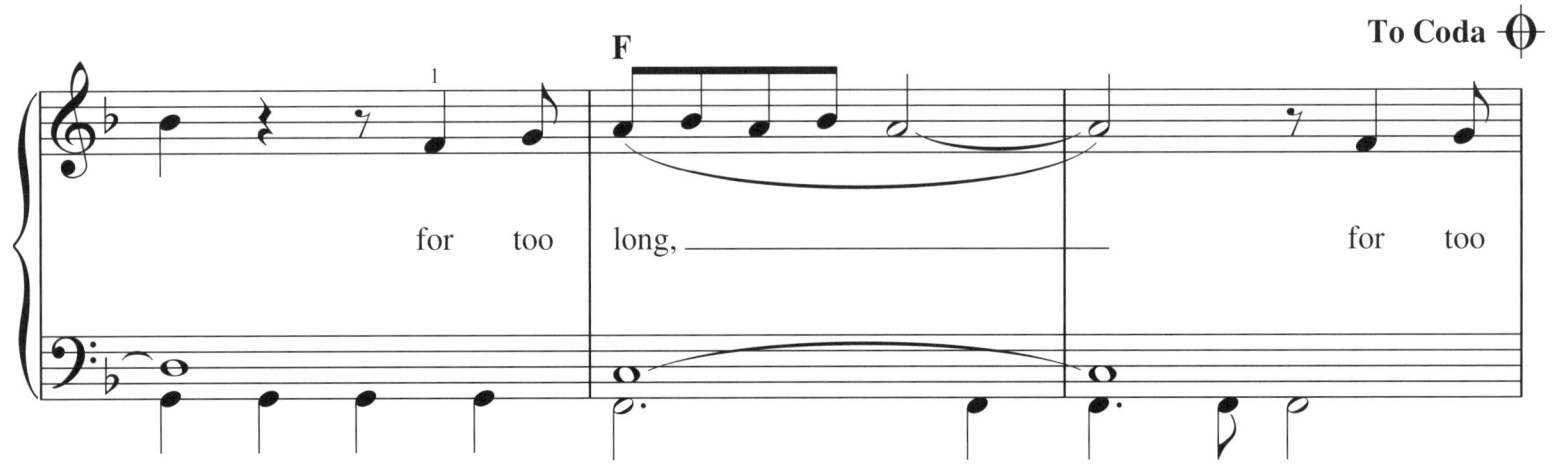

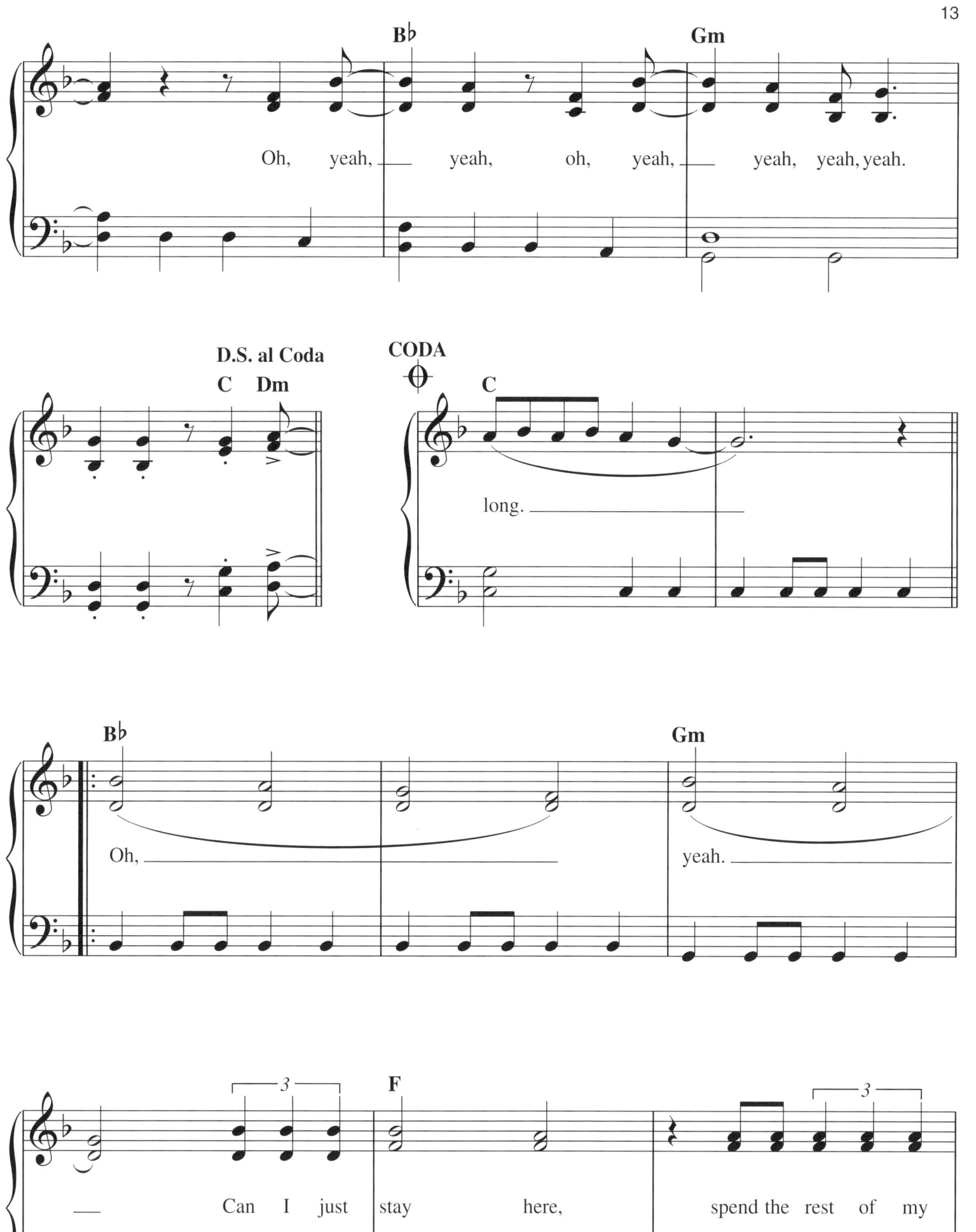

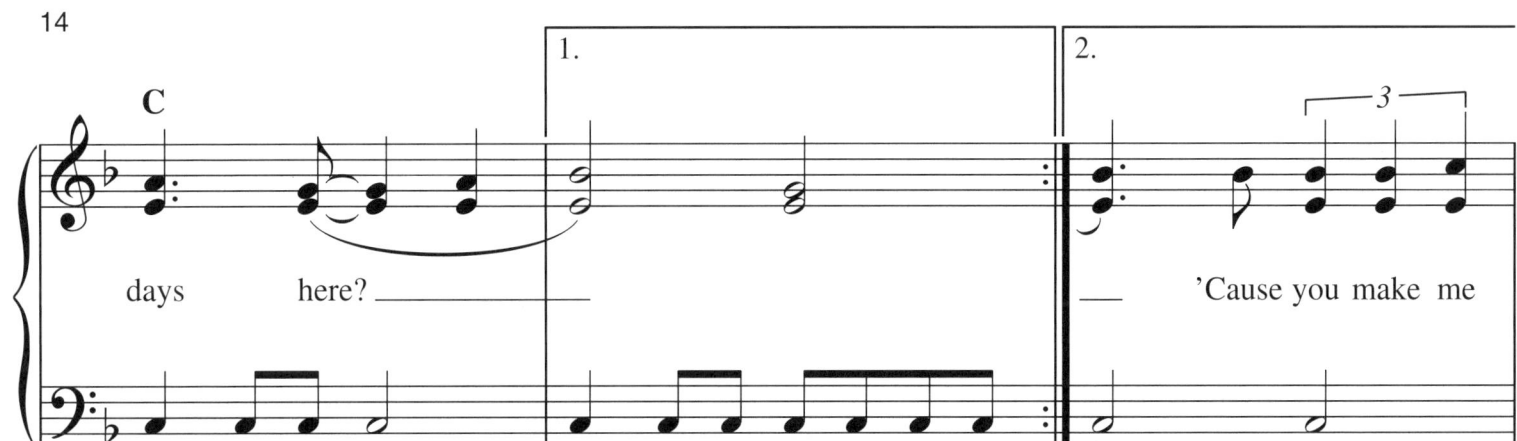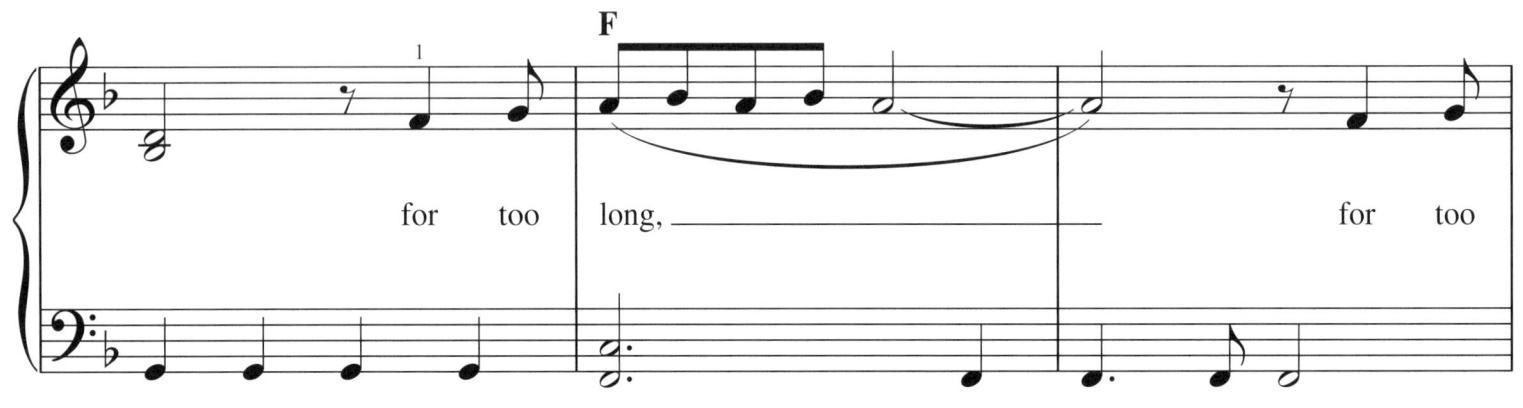

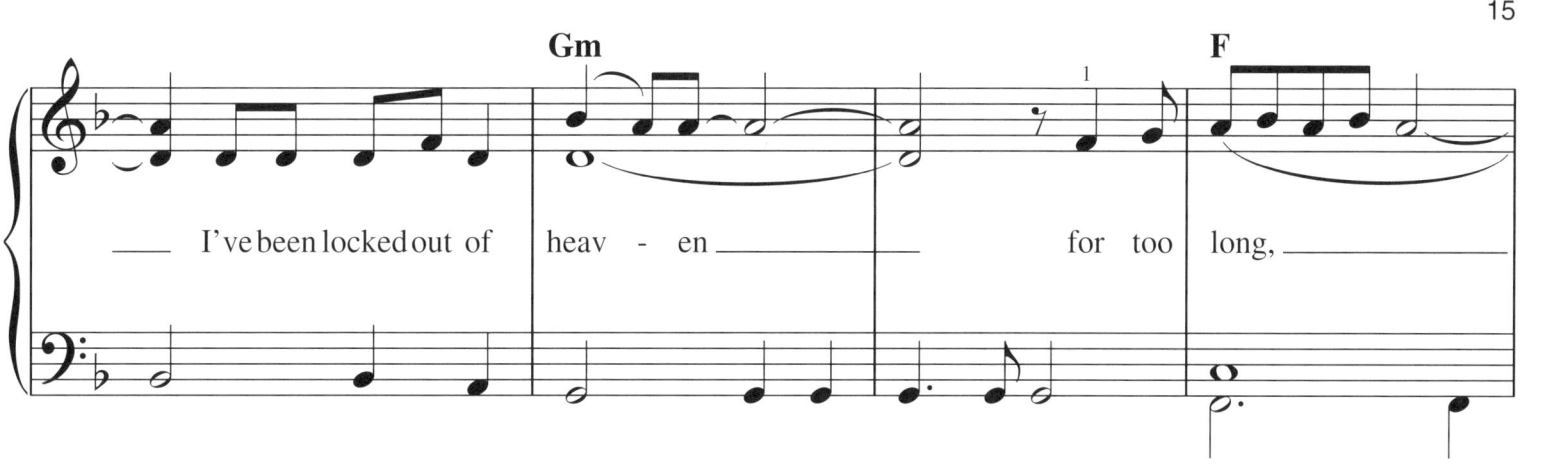
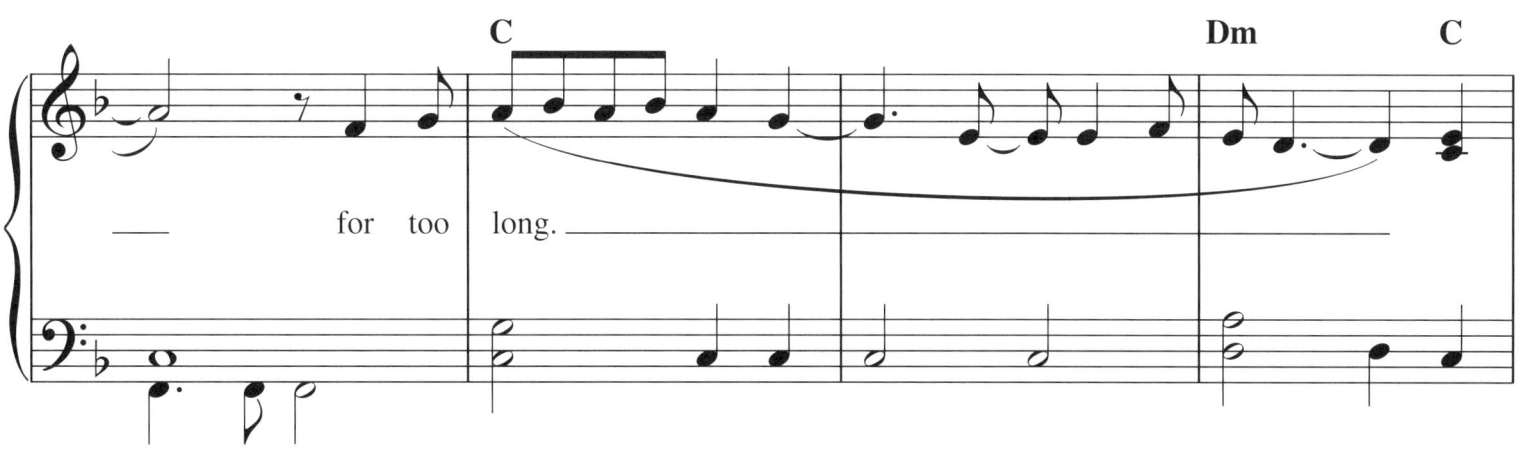

GORILLA

16

Words and Music by BRUNO MARS, ARI LEVINE and PHILIP LAWRENCE

© 2012 BMG GOLD SONGS, MARS FORCE MUSIC, UNIVERSAL MUSIC CORP., TOY PLANE MUSIC,
NORTHSIDE INDEPENDENT MUSIC PUBLISHING LLC, THOU ART THE HUNGER, WB MUSIC CORP., ROC NATION MUSIC and MUSIC FAMAMANEM
All Rights for BMG GOLD SONGS and MARS FORCE MUSIC Administered by BMG RIGHTS MANAGEMENT (US) LLC
All Rights for TOY PLANE MUSIC Controlled and Administered by UNIVERSAL MUSIC CORP.
All Rights for THOU ART THE HUNGER Administered by NORTHSIDE INDEPENDENT MUSIC PUBLISHING LLC
All Rights for ROC NATION MUSIC and MUSIC FAMAMANEM Administered by WB MUSIC CORP.
All Rights Reserved   Used by Permission

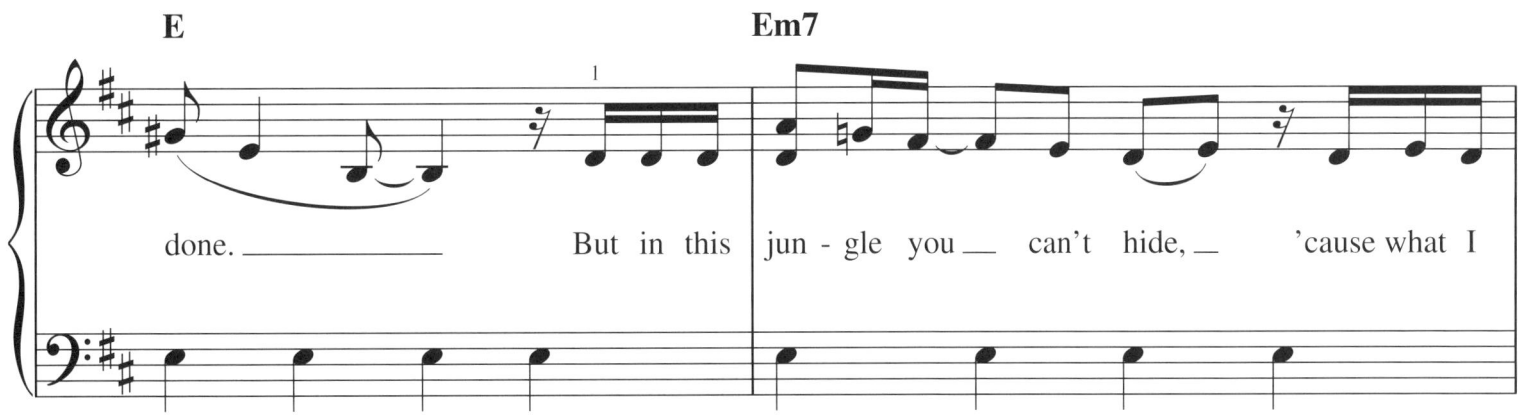

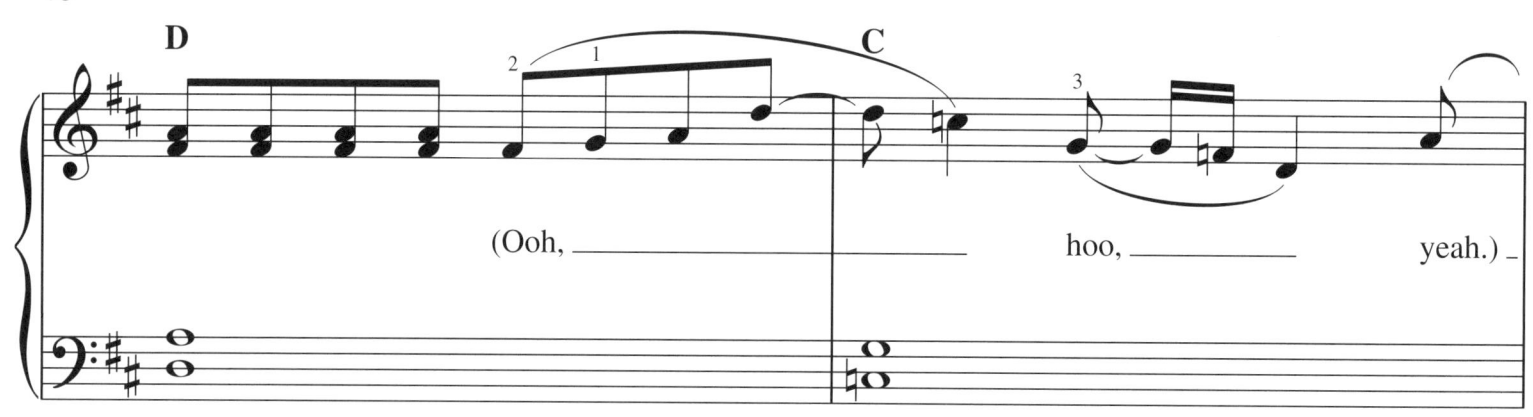

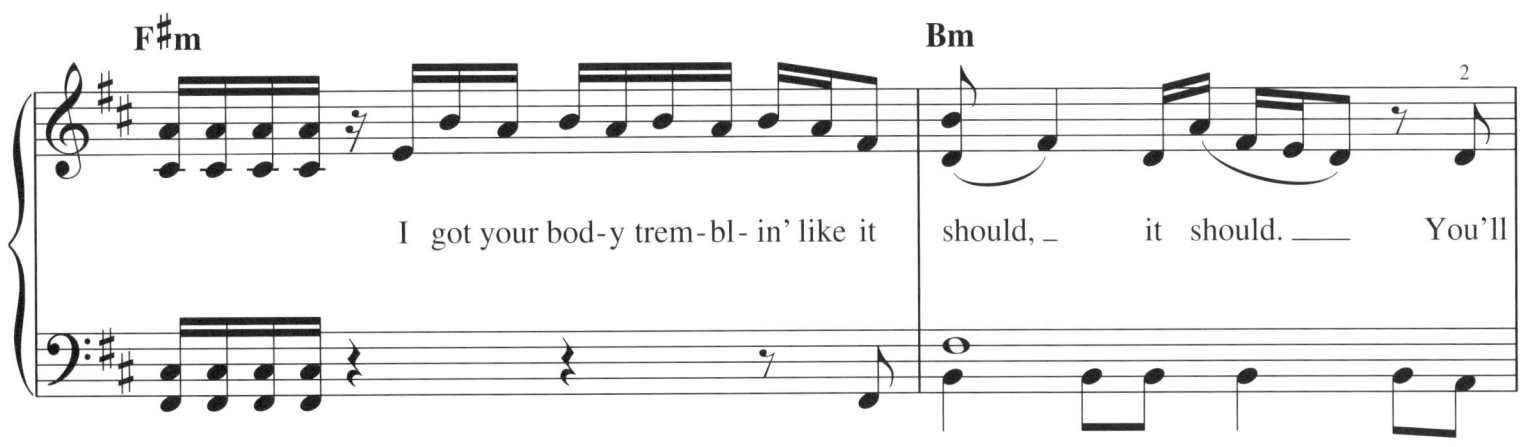
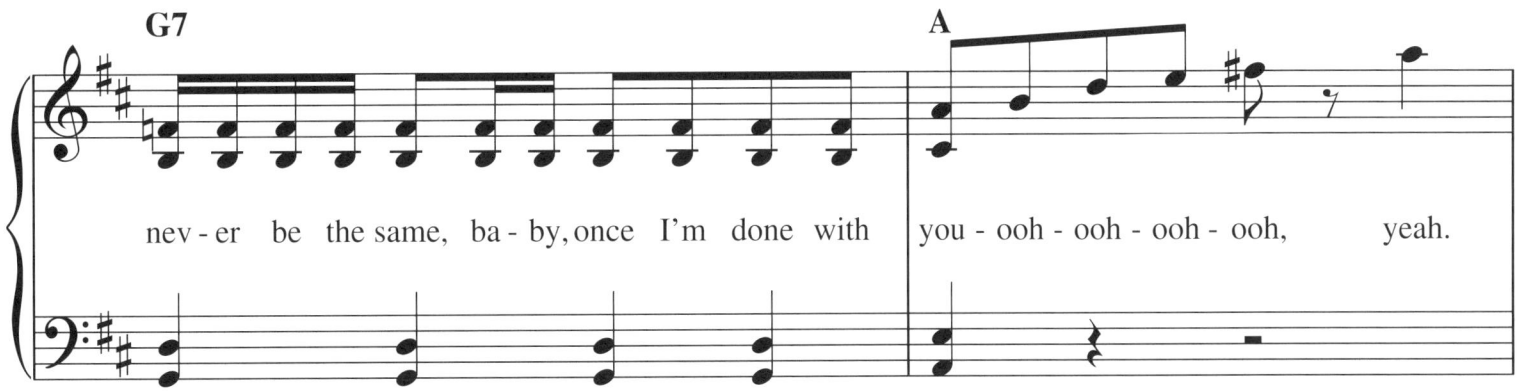
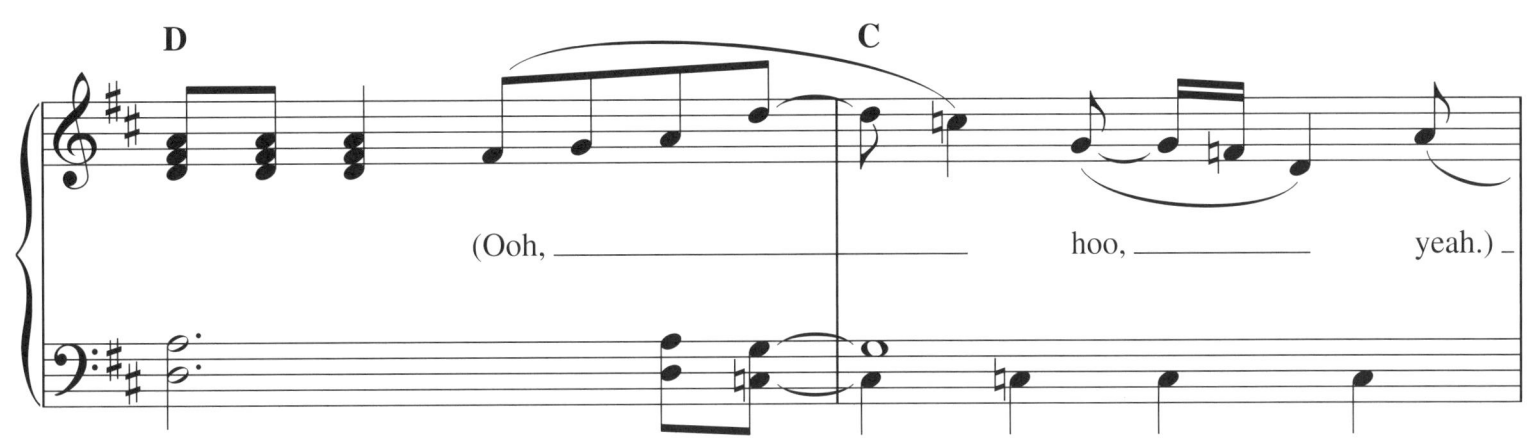

Additional Lyrics

Yeah, got a fistful of your hair,
But you don't look like you're scared;
You just smile and tell me, "Daddy, it's yours,"
'Cause you know how I like it. You's a dirty little lover.

If the neighbors call the cops,
Call the sheriff, call the S.W.A.T.,
We don't stop. We keep rockin' while
They're knockin' on our door.
And you're screamin', "Give it to me baby,
Give it to me ****."

Ooh, look what you're doin', look what you've done.
But in this jungle you can't run, 'cause what I....

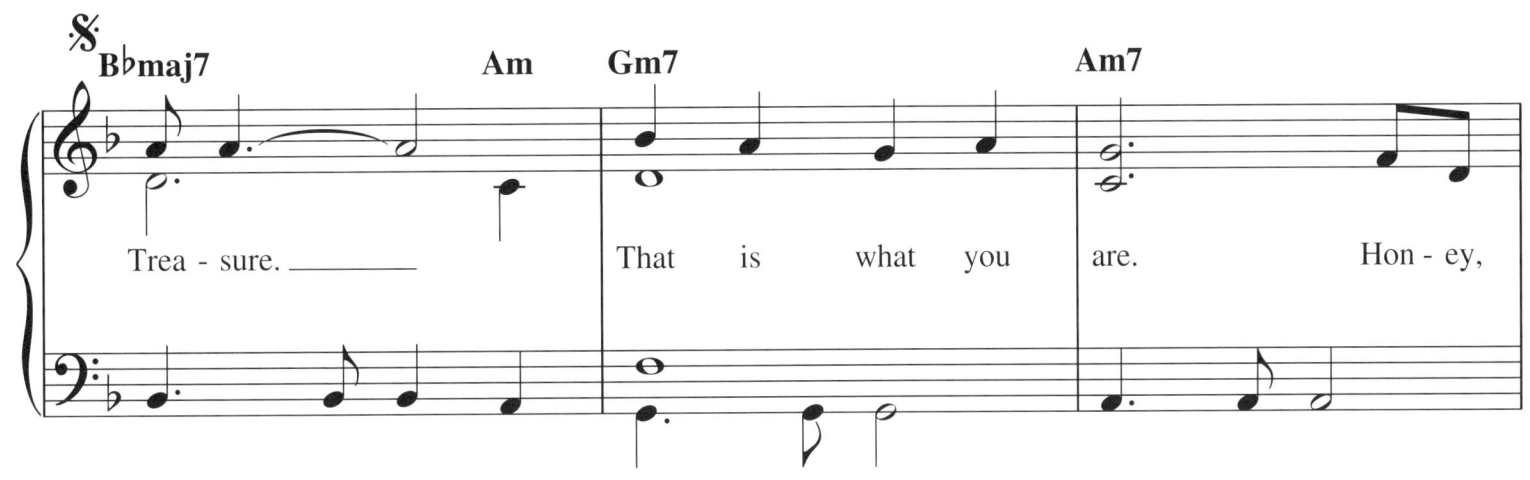

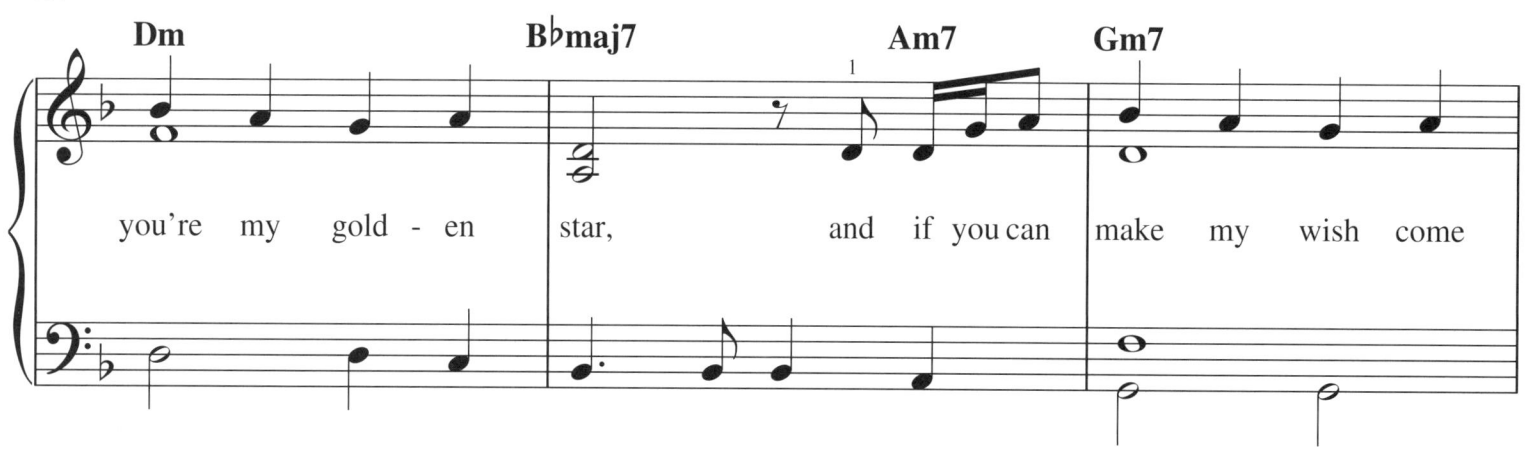

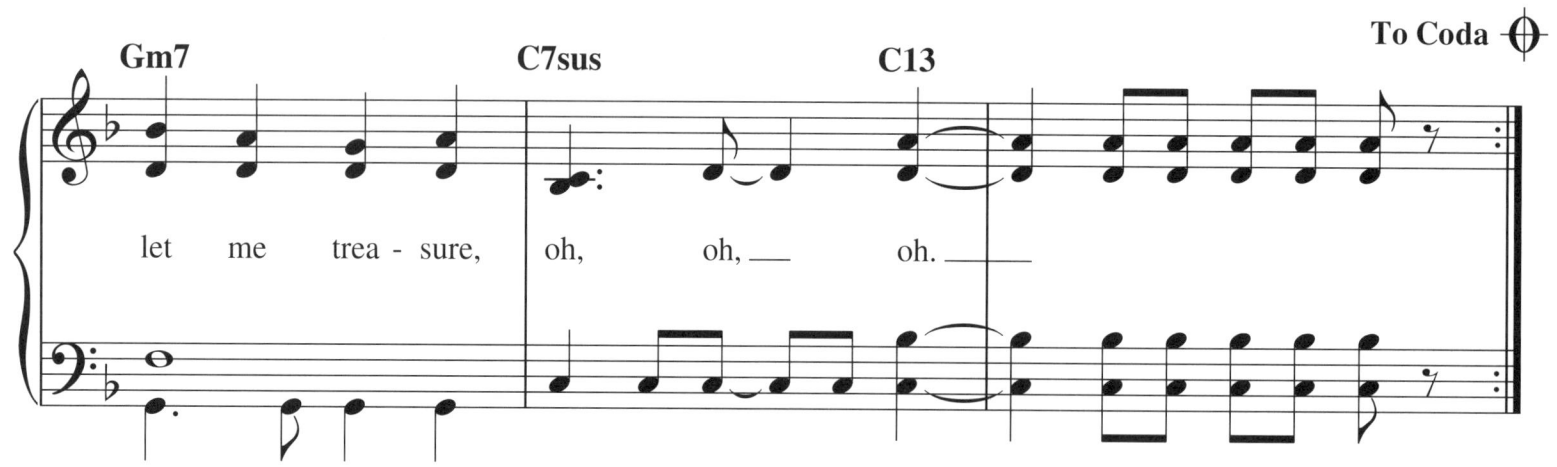

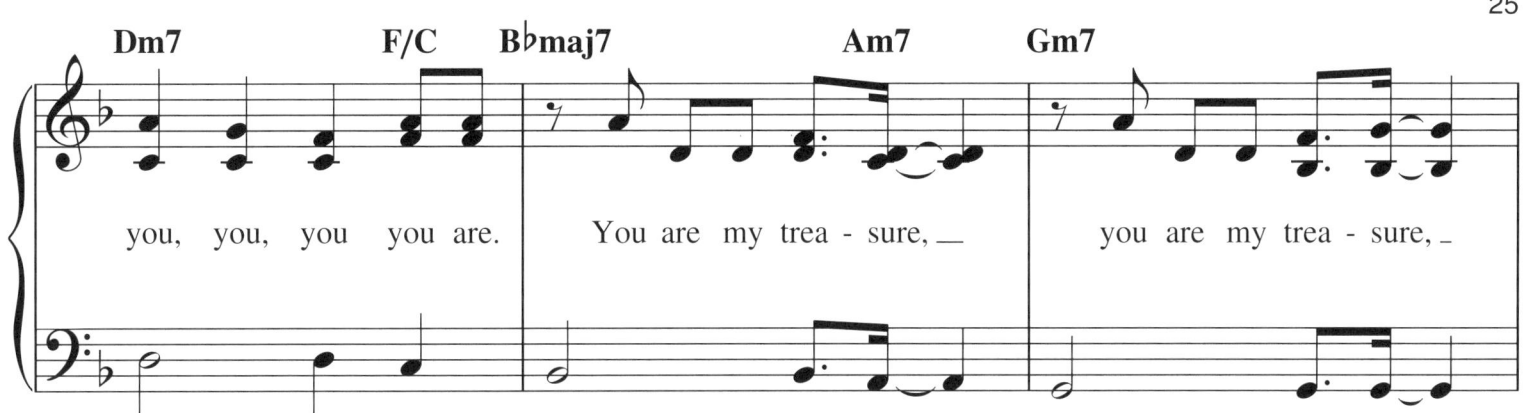

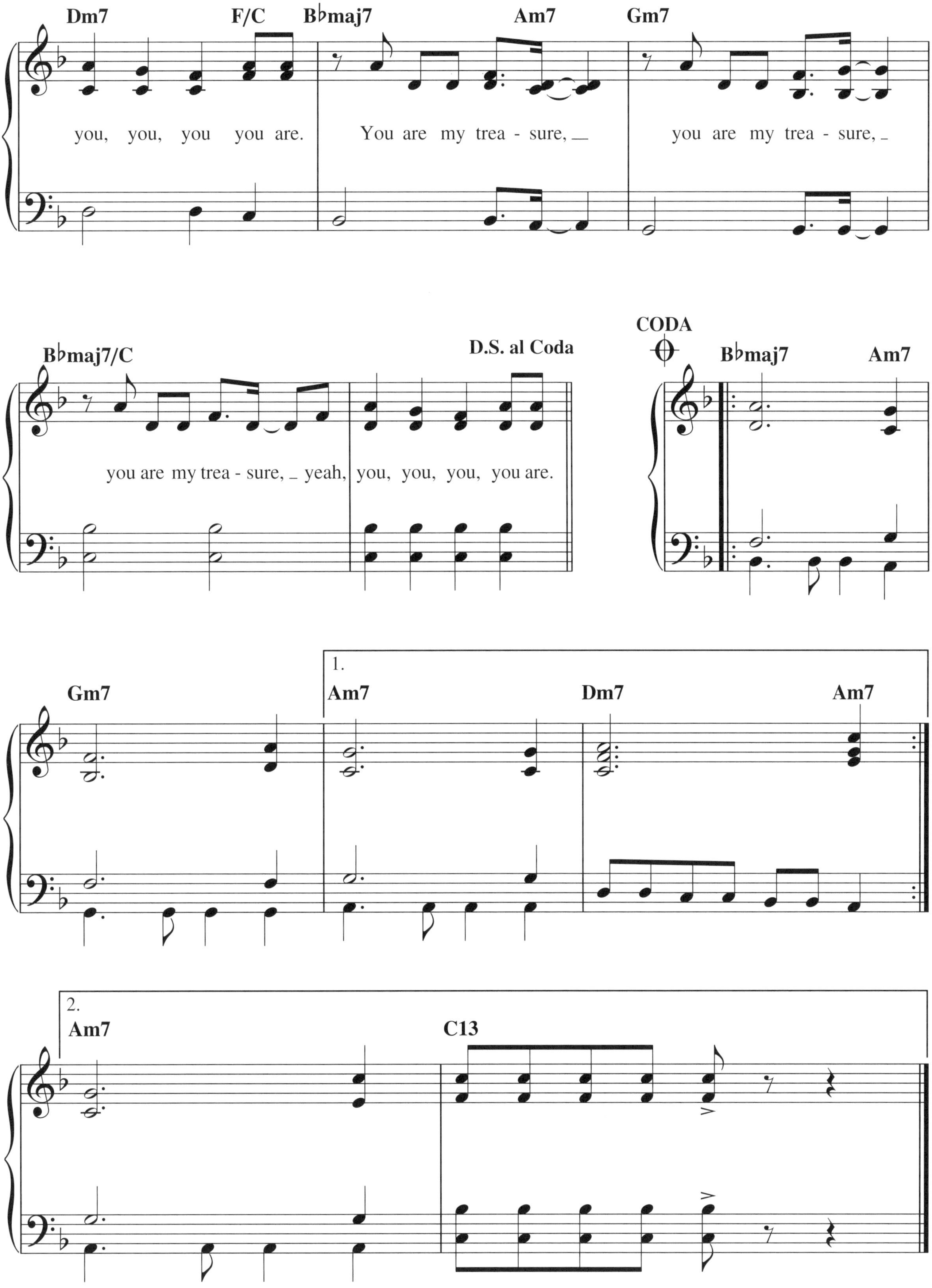
Dm7
F/C
B♭maj7
Am7
Gm7
you, you, you you are.
You are my trea - sure,
you are my trea - sure,
B♭maj7/C
D.S. al Coda
you are my trea - sure, yeah,
you, you, you, you are.
CODA
B♭maj7
Am7
Gm7
1.
Am7
Dm7
Am7
2.
Am7
C13

MOONSHINE

Words and Music by BRUNO MARS,
ARI LEVINE, PHILIP LAWRENCE,
JEFF BHASKER, ANDREW WYATT
and MARK RONSON

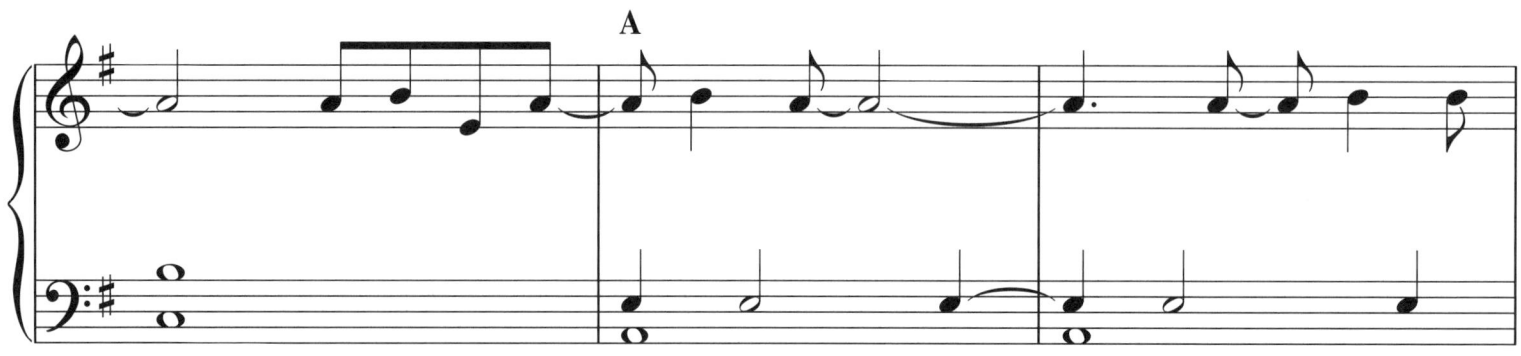

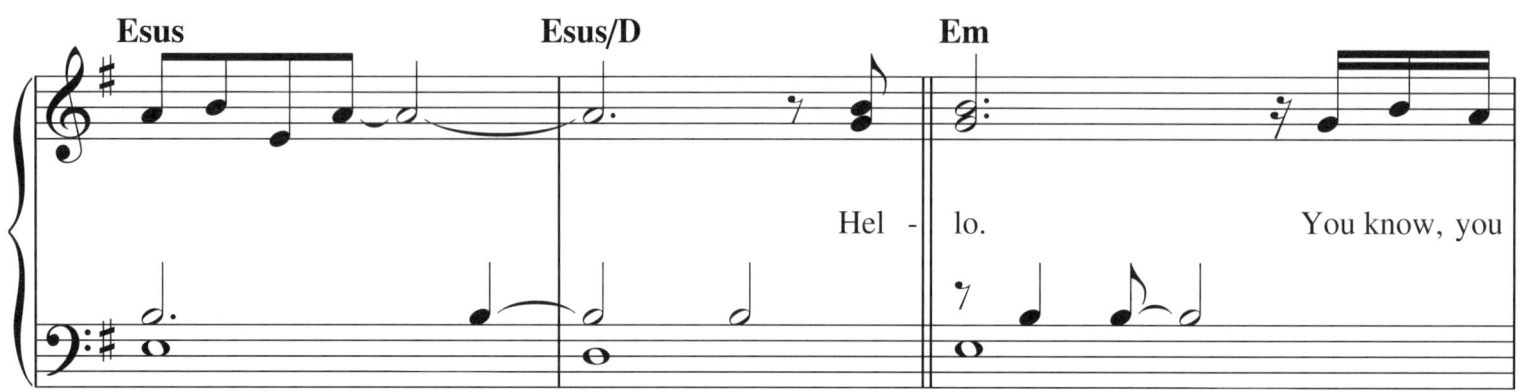

© 2012 BMG GOLD SONGS, MARS FORCE MUSIC, UNIVERSAL MUSIC CORP., TOY PLANE MUSIC, NORTHSIDE INDEPENDENT MUSIC PUBLISHING LLC, THOU ART THE HUNGER,
WB MUSIC CORP., ROC NATION MUSIC, MUSIC FAMAMANEM, SONY/ATV MUSIC PUBLISHING LLC, WAY ABOVE MUSIC, DOWNTOWN DMP SONGS and EMI MUSIC PUBLISHING LTD.
All Rights for BMG GOLD SONGS and MARS FORCE MUSIC Administered by BMG RIGHTS MANAGEMENT (US) LLC
All Rights for TOY PLANE MUSIC Controlled and Administered by UNIVERSAL MUSIC CORP.
All Rights for THOU ART THE HUNGER Administered by NORTHSIDE INDEPENDENT MUSIC PUBLISHING LLC
All Rights for ROC NATION MUSIC and MUSIC FAMAMANEM Administered by WB MUSIC CORP.
All Rights for SONY/ATV MUSIC PUBLISHING LLC and WAY ABOVE MUSIC Administered by SONY/ATV MUSIC PUBLISHING LLC, 8 Music Square West, Nashville, TN 37203
All Rights for DOWNTOWN DMP SONGS Administered by DOWNTOWN MUSIC PUBLISHING LLC
All Rights for EMI MUSIC PUBLISHING LTD. in the U.S. and Canada Controlled and Administered by EMI Blackwood Music Inc.
All Rights Reserved   Used by Permission

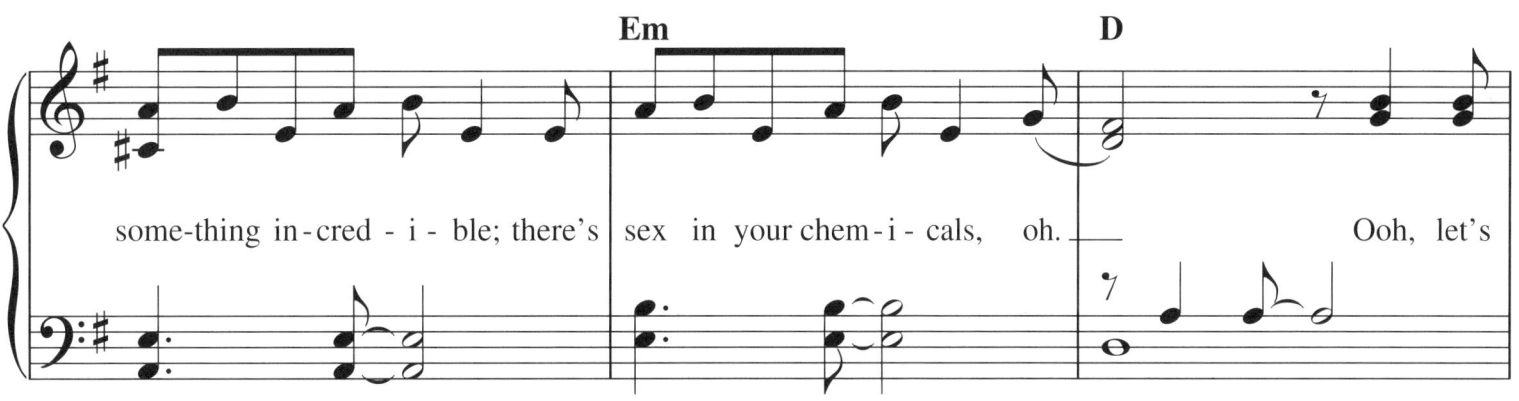

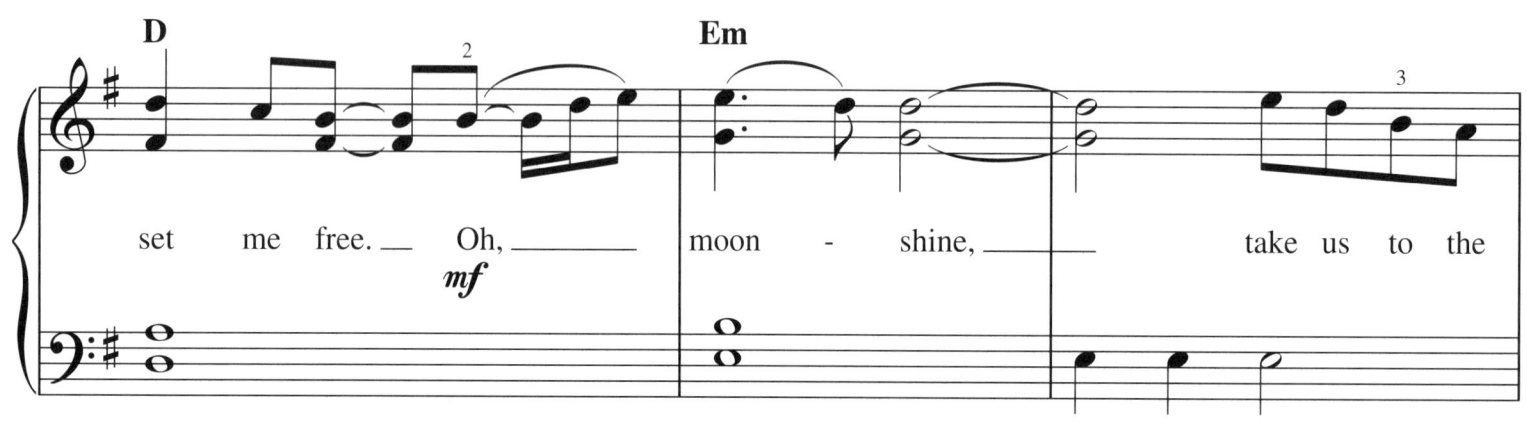

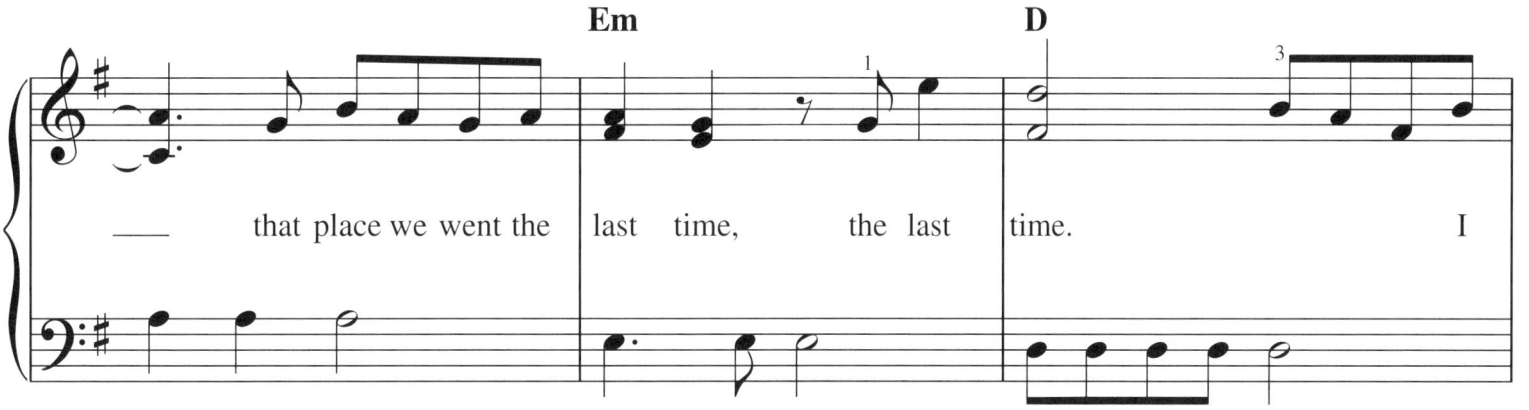

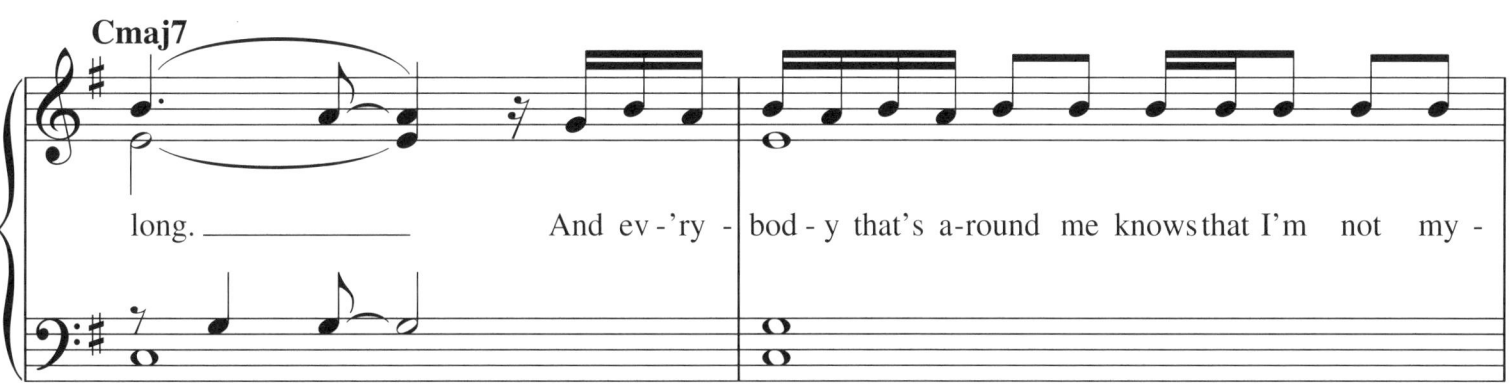

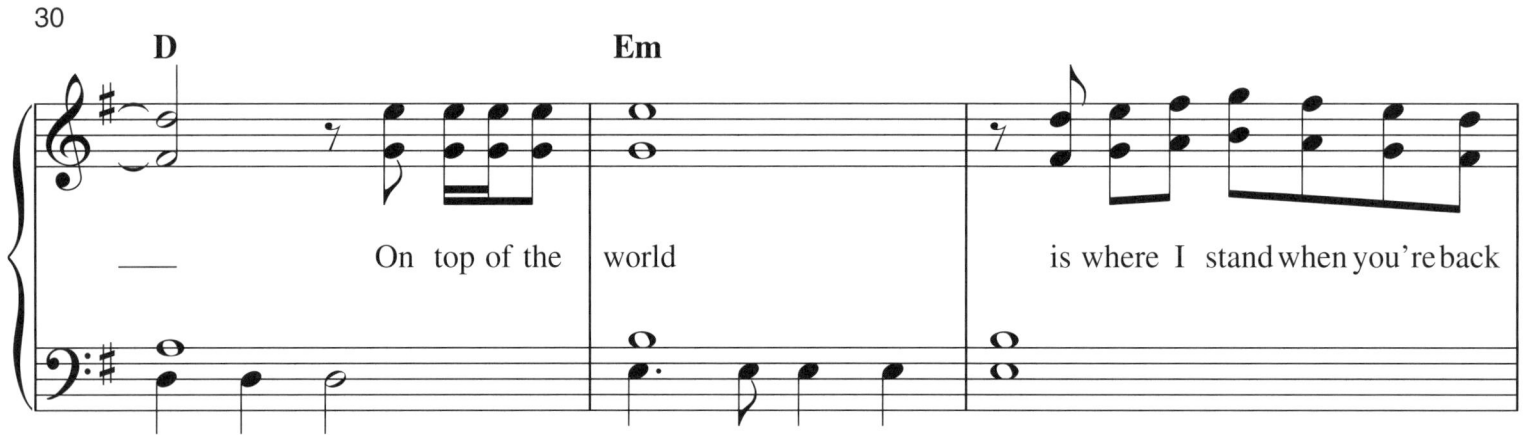

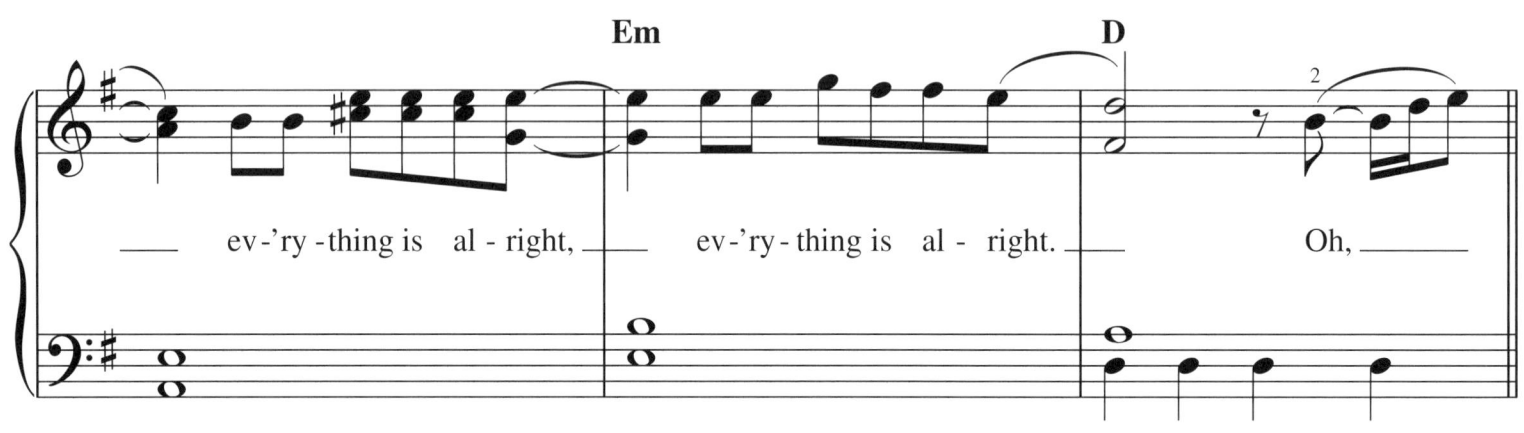

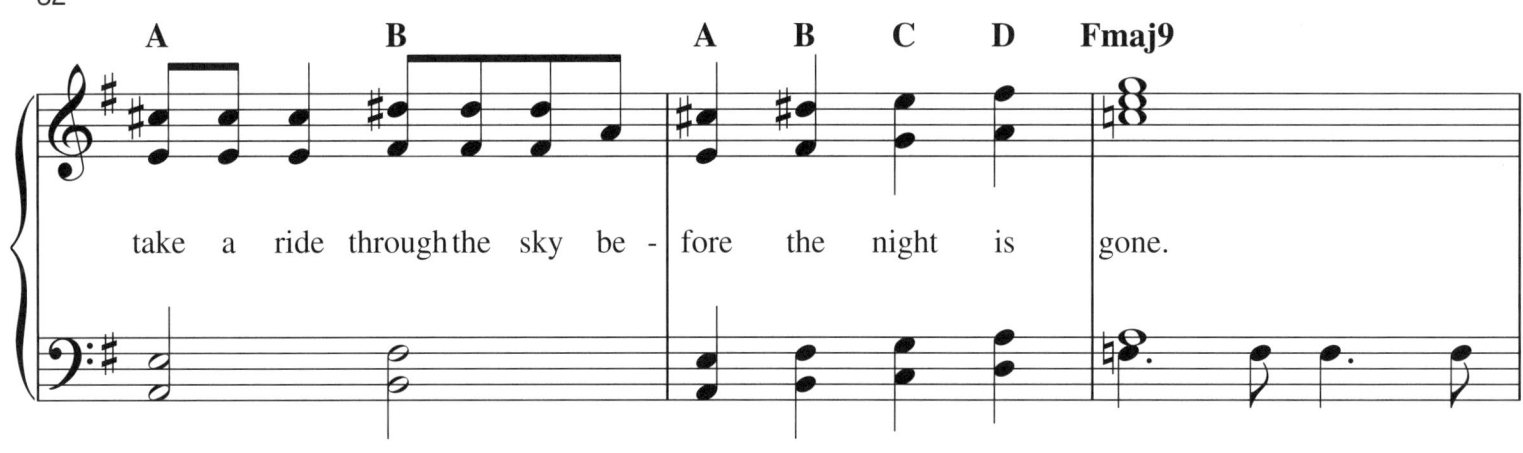
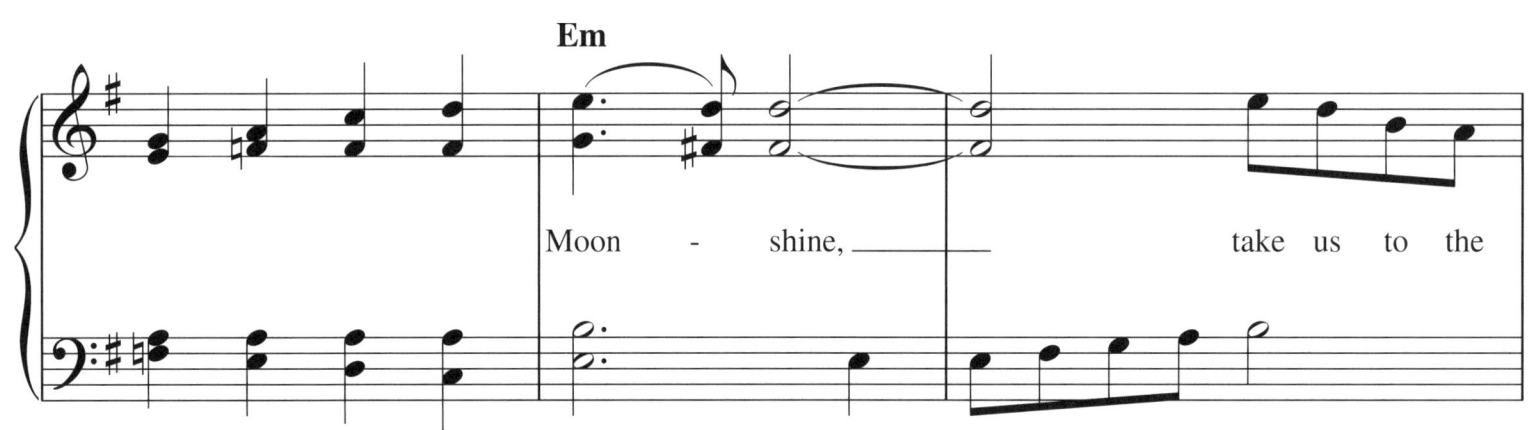

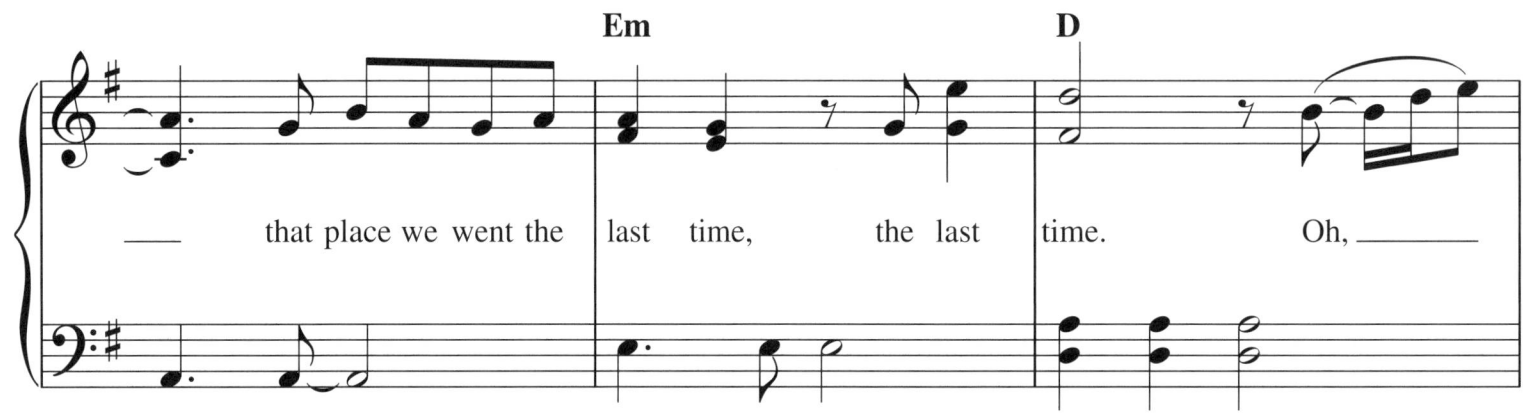

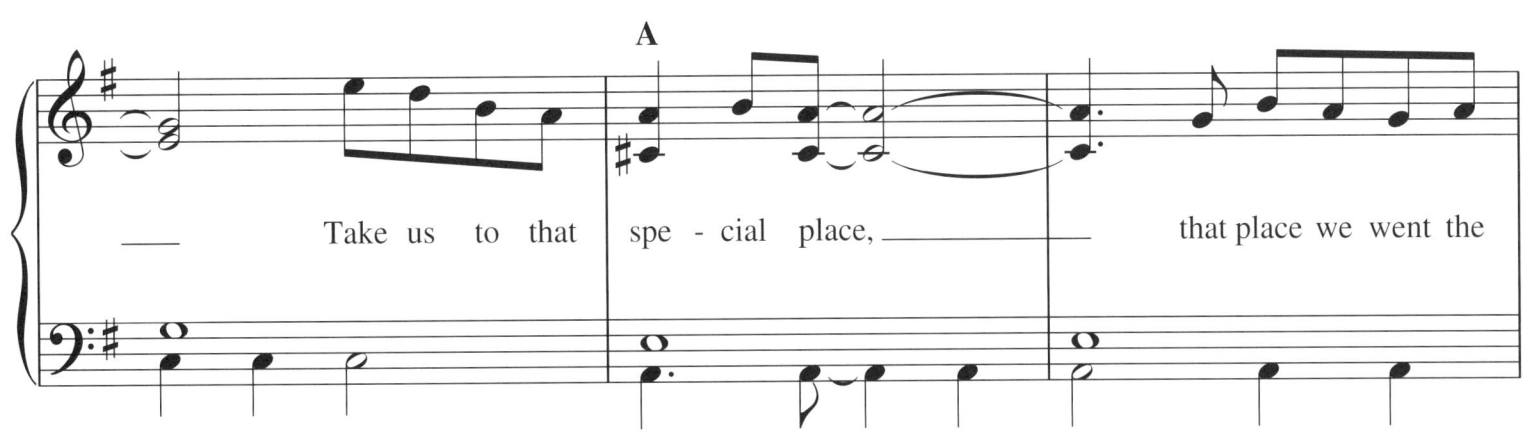
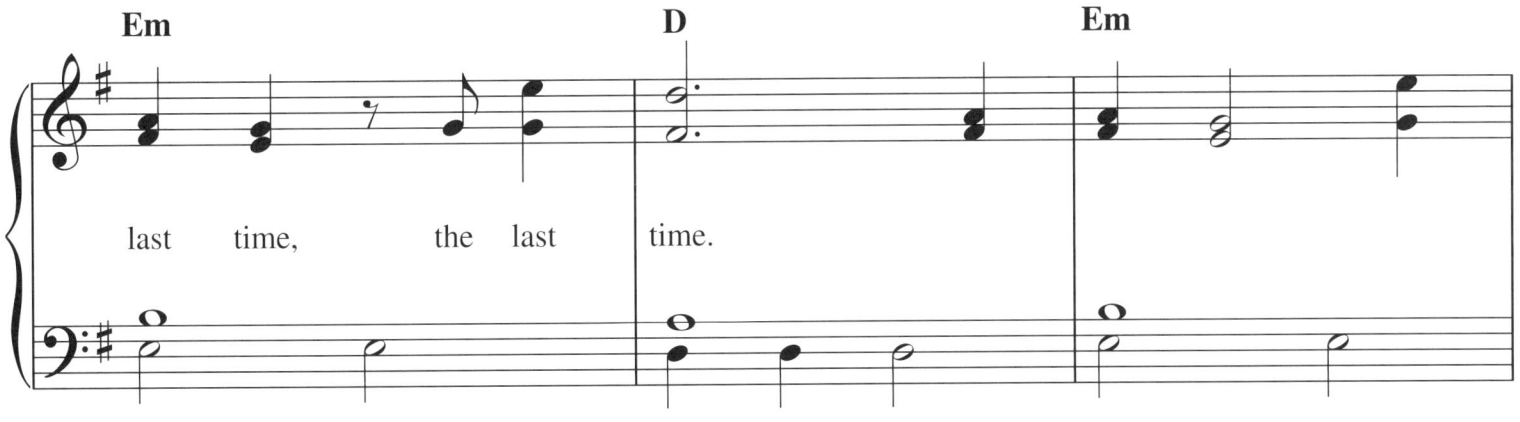
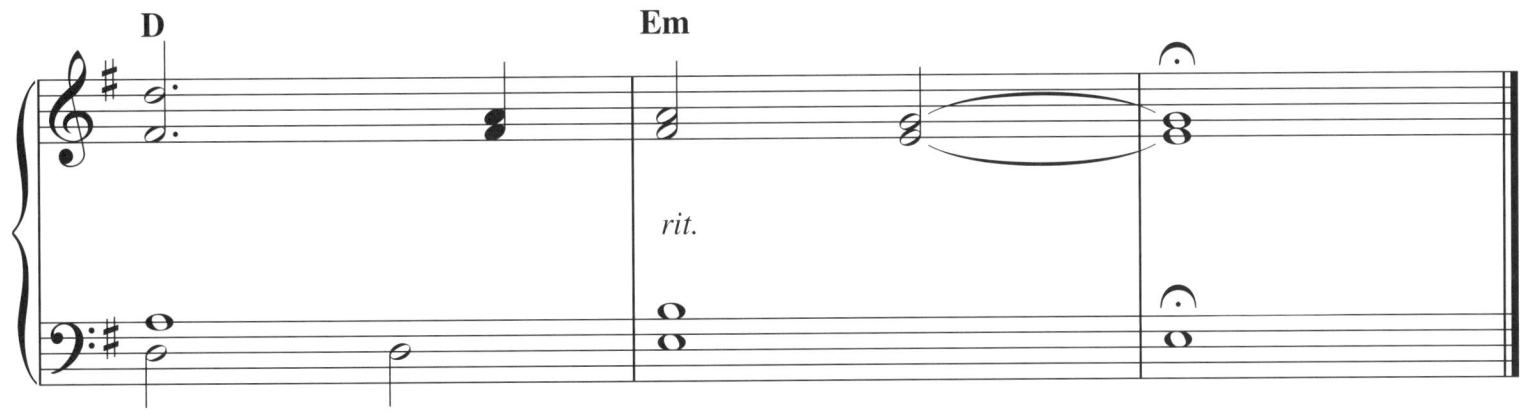

WHEN I WAS YOUR MAN

Words and Music by BRUNO MARS,
ARI LEVINE, PHILIP LAWRENCE
and ANDREW WYATT

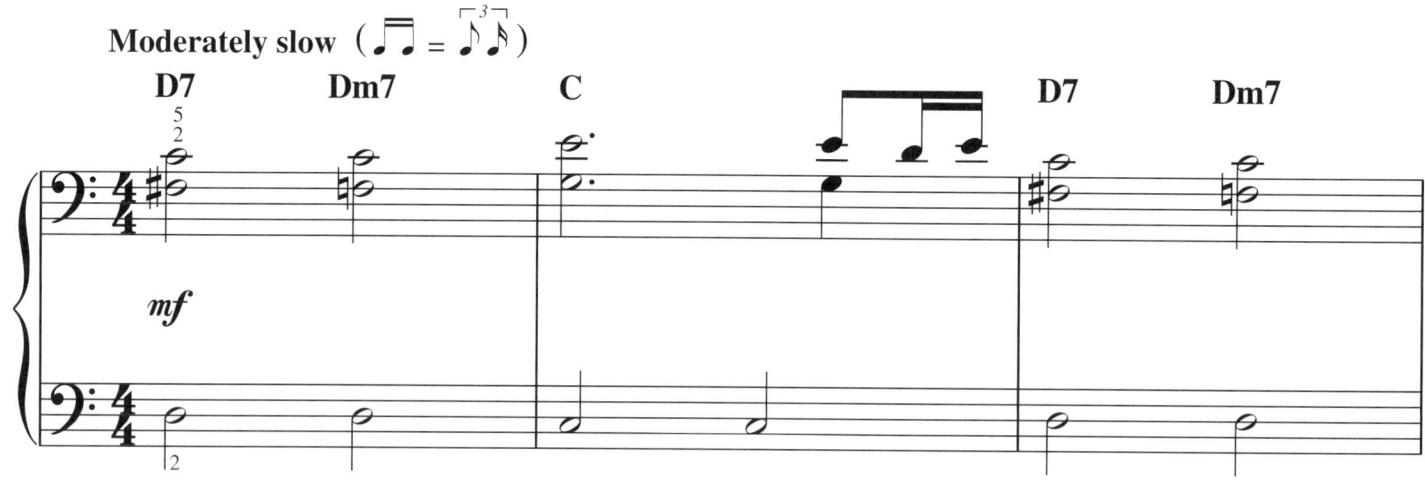

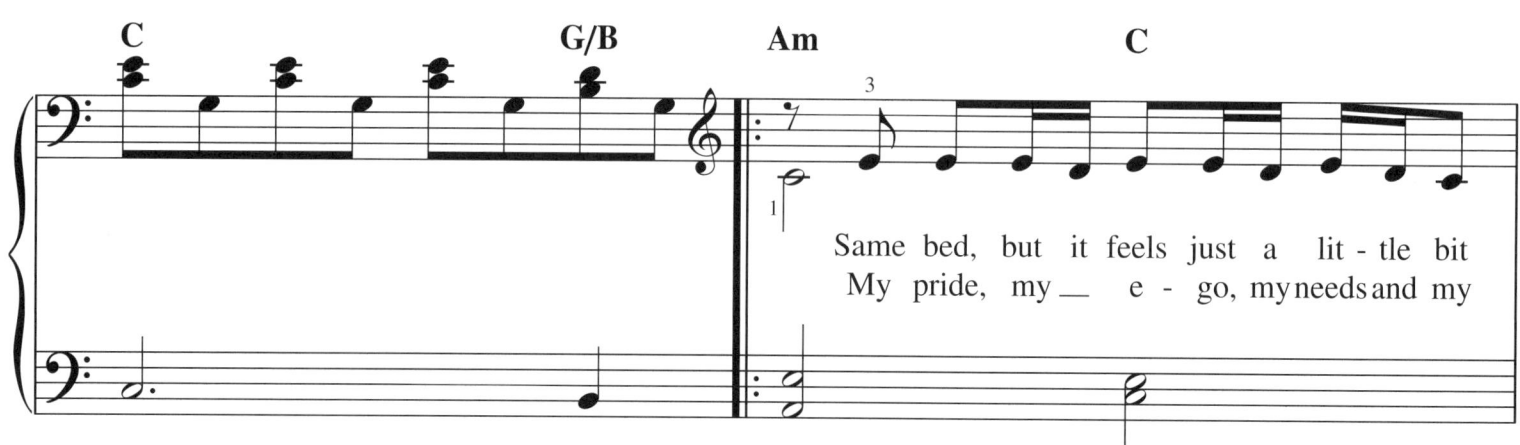

© 2012 BMG GOLD SONGS, MARS FORCE MUSIC, UNIVERSAL MUSIC CORP., TOY PLANE MUSIC, NORTHSIDE INDEPENDENT MUSIC PUBLISHING LLC,
THOU ART THE HUNGER, WB MUSIC CORP., ROC NATION MUSIC, MUSIC FAMAMANEM and DOWNTOWN DMP SONGS
All Rights for BMG GOLD SONGS and MARS FORCE MUSIC Administered by BMG RIGHTS MANAGEMENT (US) LLC
All Rights for TOY PLANE MUSIC Controlled and Administered by UNIVERSAL MUSIC CORP.
All Rights for THOU ART THE HUNGER Administered by NORTHSIDE INDEPENDENT MUSIC PUBLISHING LLC
All Rights for ROC NATION MUSIC and MUSIC FAMAMANEM Administered by WB MUSIC CORP.
All Rights for DOWNTOWN DMP SONGS Administered by DOWNTOWN MUSIC PUBLISHING LLC
All Rights Reserved   Used by Permission

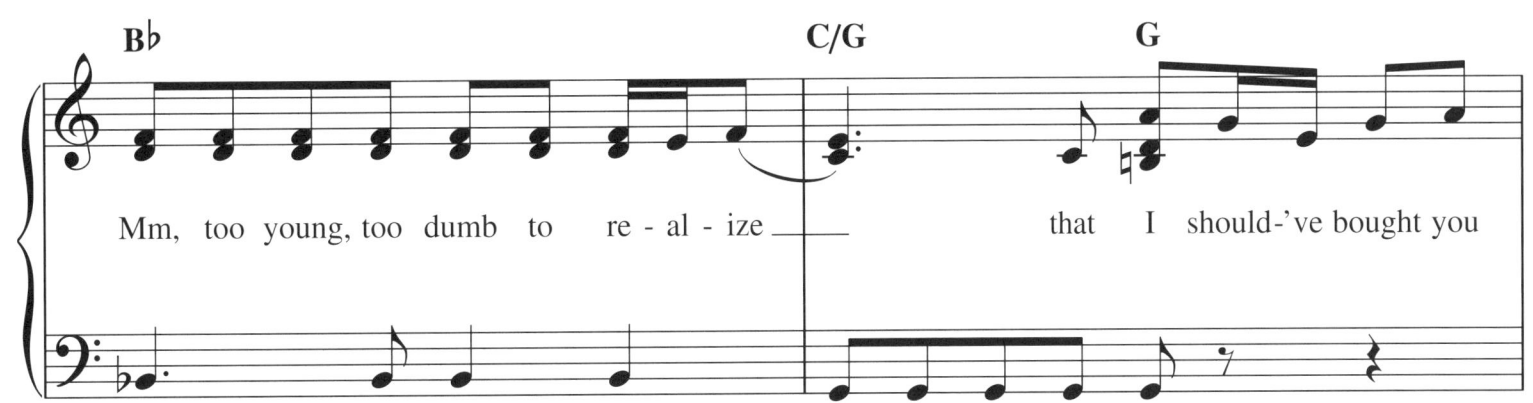

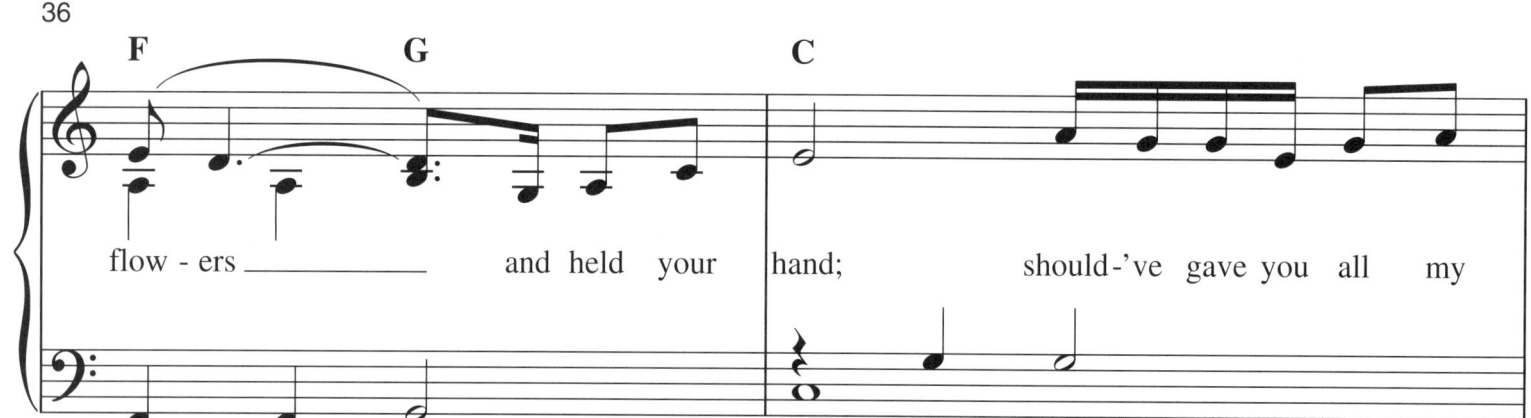
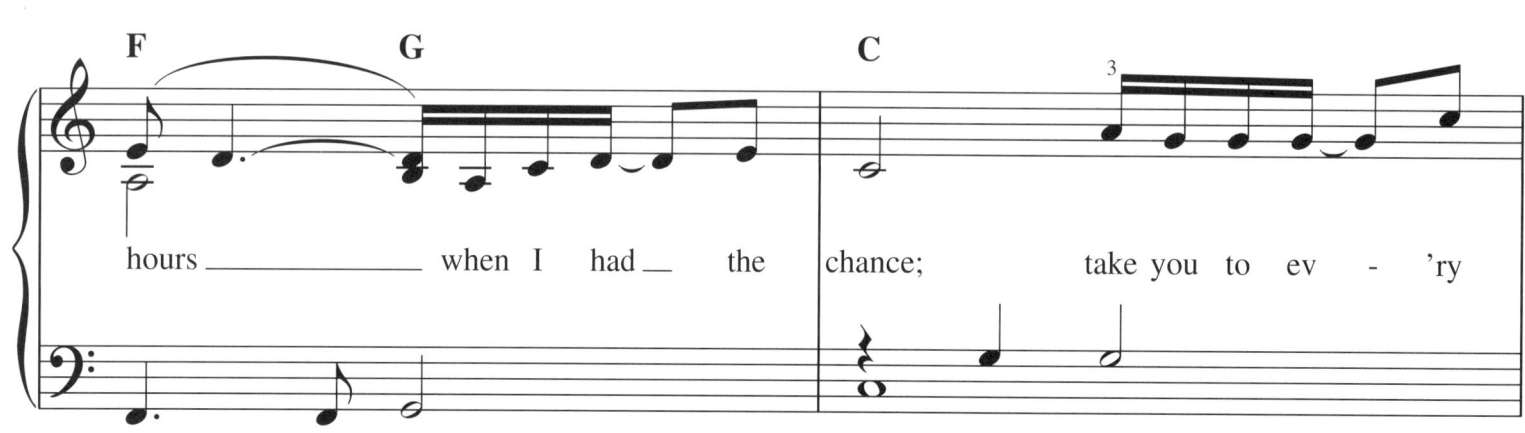
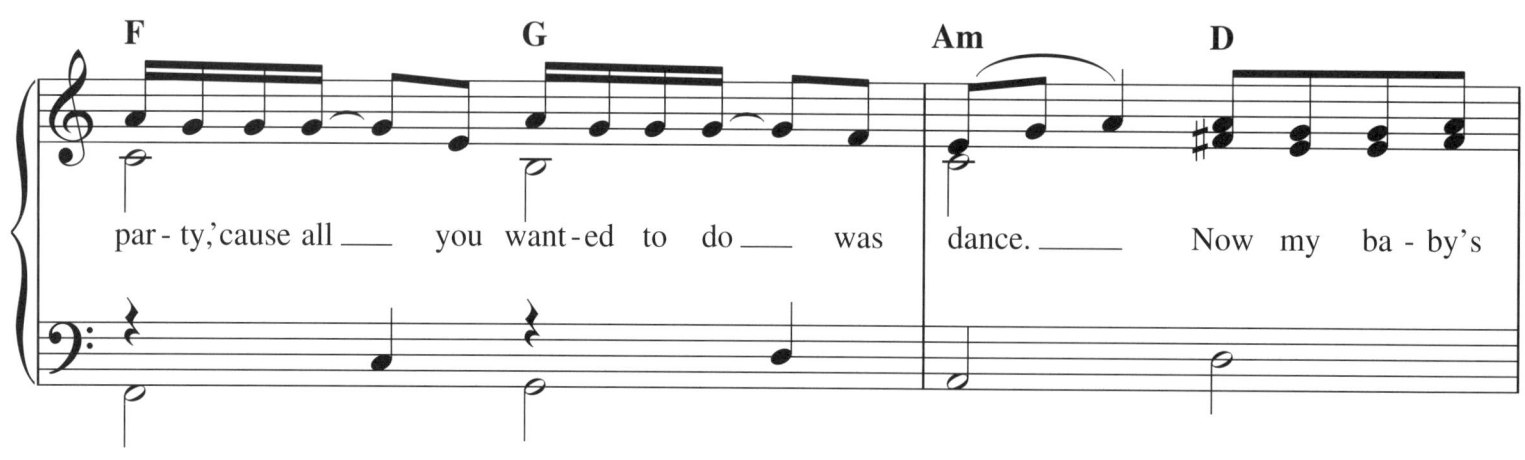
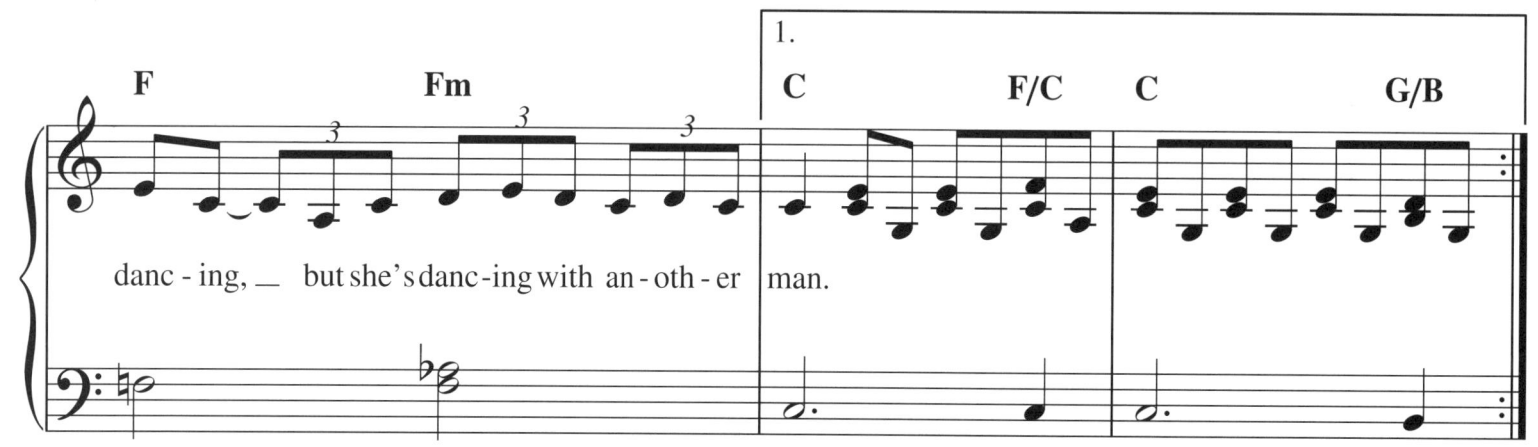

2.
C F G
man. Al-though it hurts, I'll be the first to say that I was
C G/B Am Em/G D7/F♯
wrong. Oh, I know I'm prob-'ly much too late to try and a-
Dm/F G
pol-o-gize for my mis-takes. But I just want you to know,
N.C. F G
I hope he buys you flow-ers; I hope he holds your

C F G
hand, give you all his hours when he has the
C F G
chance; take you to ev-'ry par - ty, 'cause I re - mem- ber how much you love
Am D F Fm
to dance; do all the things I should-'ve done when I was your
C Am F Fm C
man. Do all the things I should-'ve done when I was your man.
3
rit.

NATALIE

Words and Music by BRUNO MARS, ARI LEVINE, PHILIP LAWRENCE, PAUL EPWORTH and BENJAMINE LEVIN

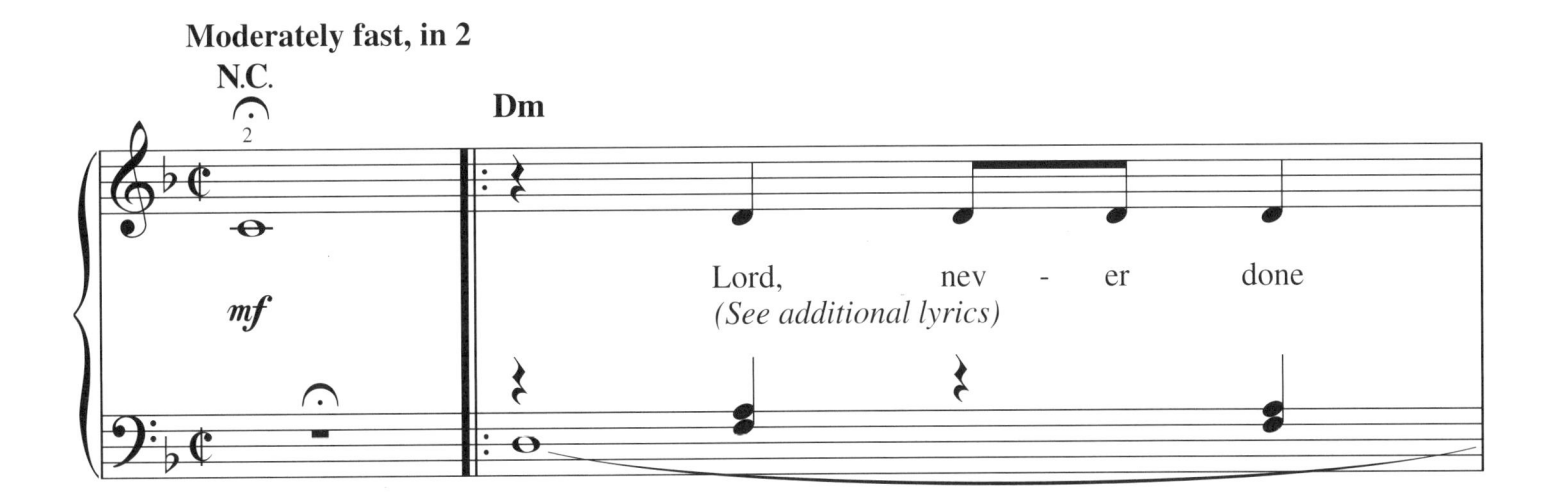

Moderately fast, in 2

Lord, nev-er done (See additional lyrics) this be-fore;_ nev-er wan-na do this a-gain._ Wrong turn on a dust-y road._ I did it to my-self; I

© 2012 BMG GOLD SONGS, MARS FORCE MUSIC, UNIVERSAL MUSIC CORP., TOY PLANE MUSIC, NORTHSIDE INDEPENDENT MUSIC PUBLISHING LLC, THOU ART THE HUNGER, WB MUSIC CORP., ROC NATION MUSIC, MUSIC FAMAMANEM, EMI MUSIC PUBLISHING LTD., MATZA BALLZACK MUSIC and WHERE DA KASZ AT?
All Rights for BMG GOLD SONGS and MARS FORCE MUSIC Administered by BMG RIGHTS MANAGEMENT (US) LLC
All Rights for TOY PLANE MUSIC Controlled and Administered by UNIVERSAL MUSIC CORP.
All Rights for THOU ART THE HUNGER Administered by NORTHSIDE INDEPENDENT MUSIC PUBLISHING LLC
All Rights for ROC NATION MUSIC and MUSIC FAMAMANEM Administered by WB MUSIC CORP.
All Rights for EMI MUSIC PUBLISHING LTD. in the U.S. and Canada Controlled and Administered by EMI APRIL MUSIC INC.
All Rights for MATZA BALLZACK MUSIC and WHERE DA KASZ AT? Administered by SONGS OF KOBALT MUSIC PUBLISHING
All Rights Reserved   Used by Permission

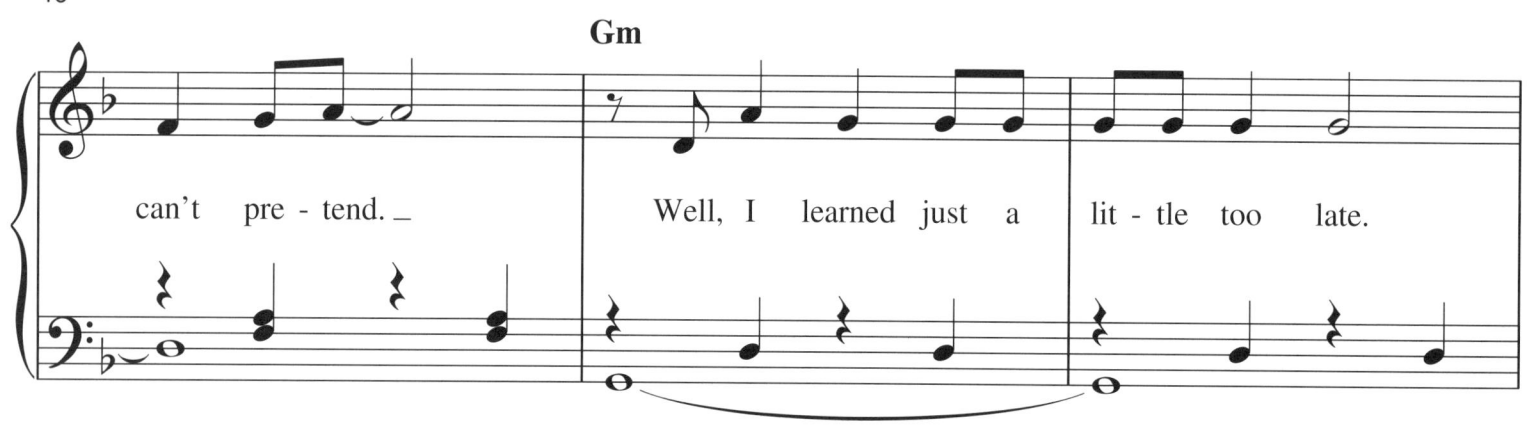

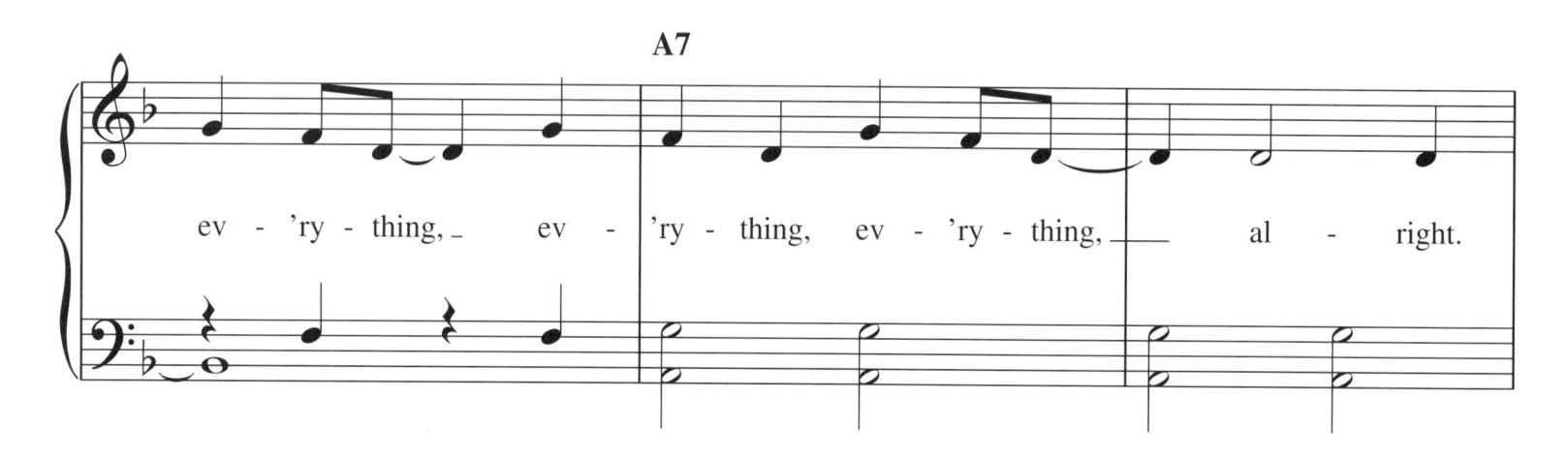

can't pre-tend. Well, I learned just a lit-tle too late.

Good God, I must-'ve been blind, 'cause she got may-be

ev-'ry-thing, ev-'ry-thing, ev-'ry-thing, al - right.

Like my dad-dy, I'm a gam-bl-ing man; nev-er been a-fraid to roll the dice. But when I put my bet on her, little Miss Snake Eyes ruined my life.

Gm

She'd better sleep with one eye open, better make sure to lock her doors,

B♭

'cause once I get my hands on her, I'm a

A7

ooh!

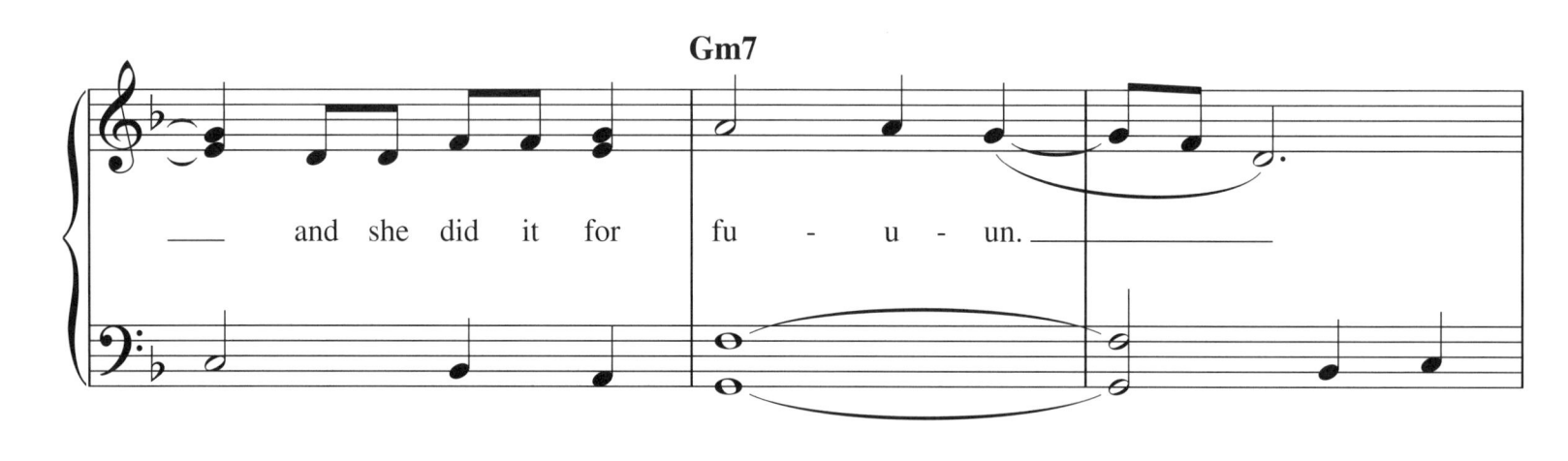

Na - ta - lie. ___ She ran a-way with all my mon - ey, ___ and she did it for fu - u - un. ___ Nat - a - lie. ___ She's prob - 'ly out there

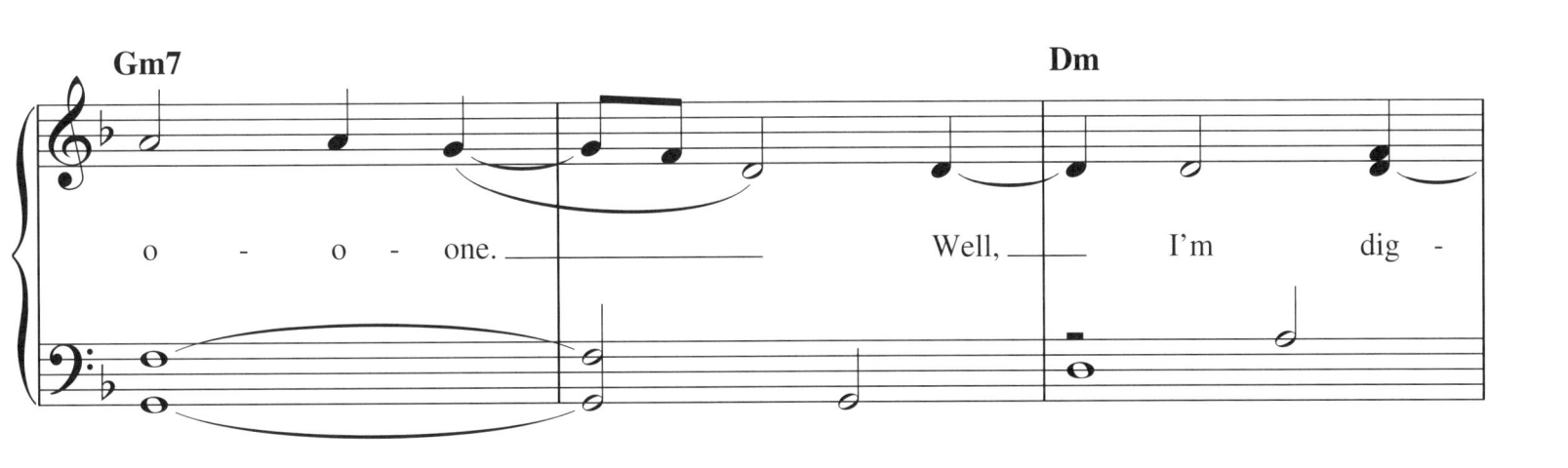

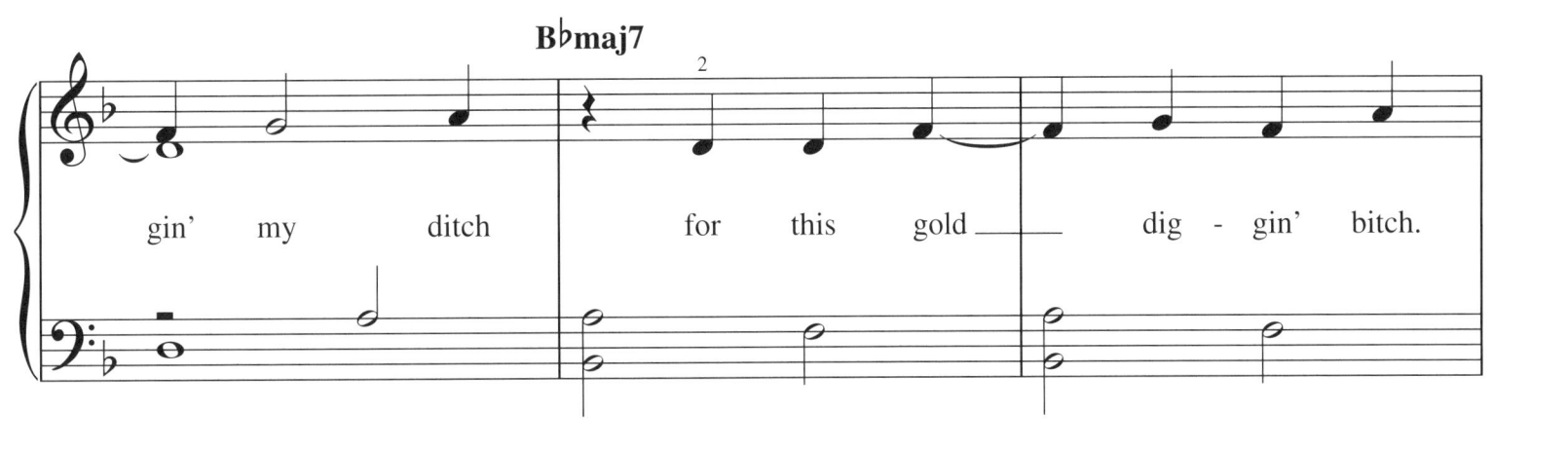

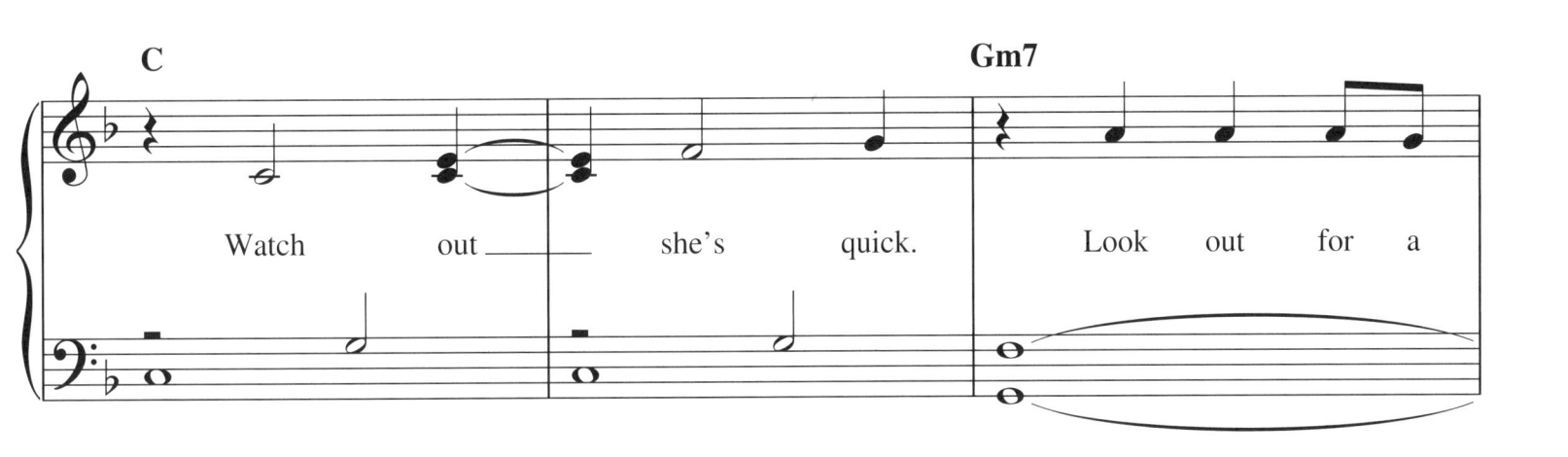

thinking it's funny, and telling ev-'ry-o - o - one. Well, I'm dig-gin' my ditch for this gold diggin' bitch. Watch out she's quick. Look out for a pret - ty lit - tle thing named Nat - a - lie. If you

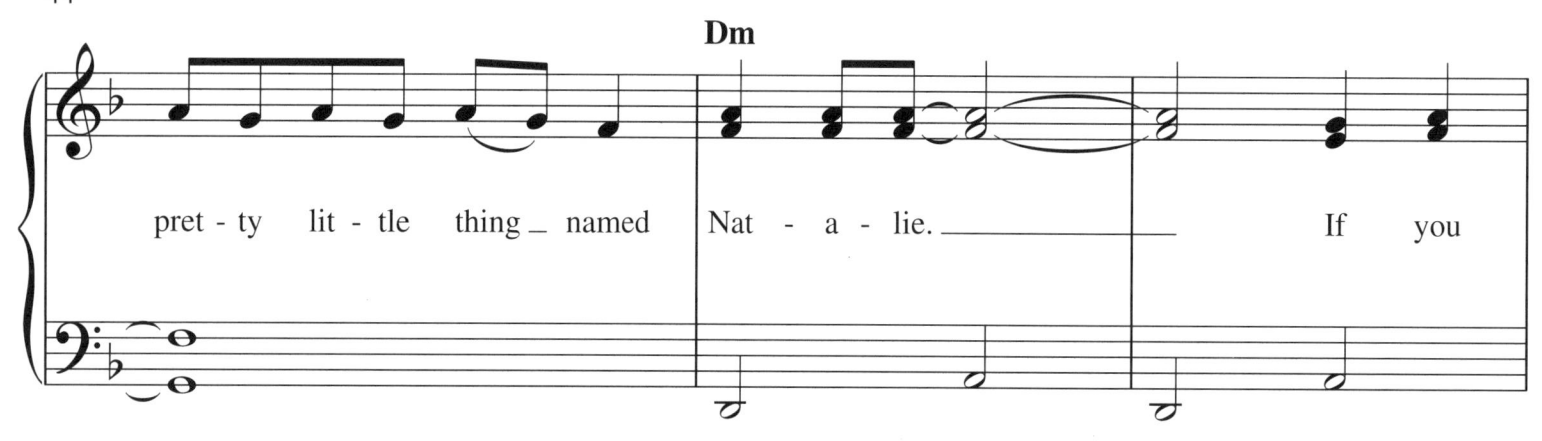

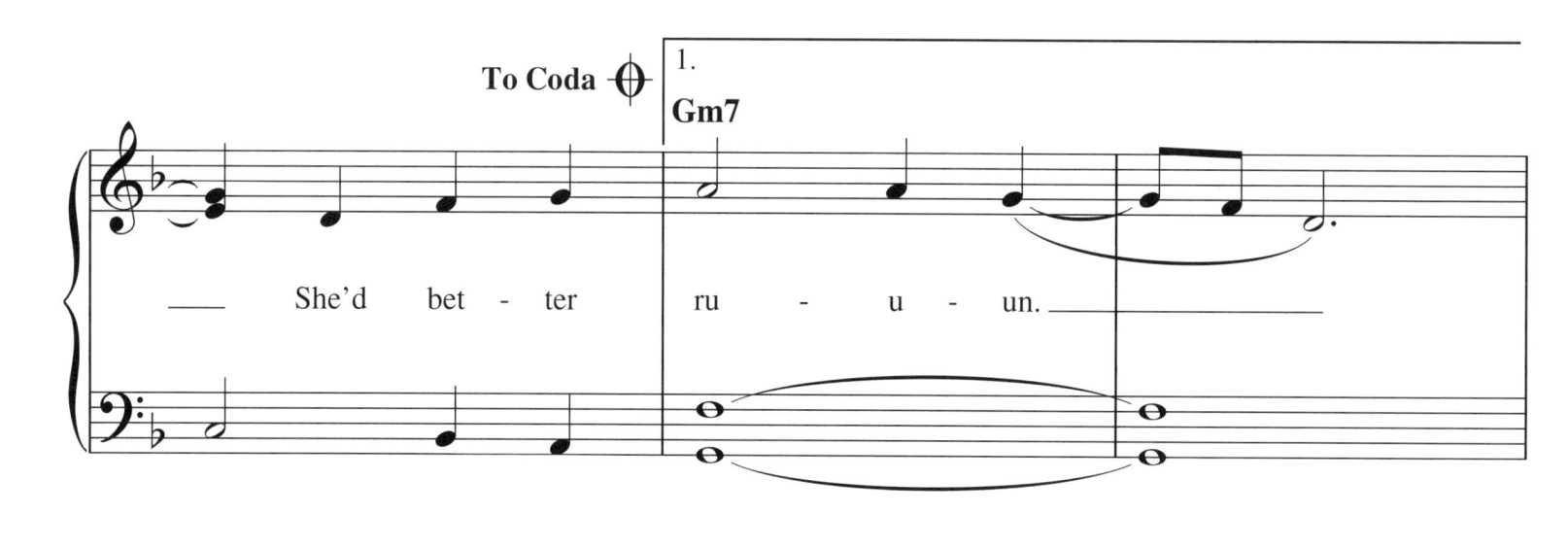

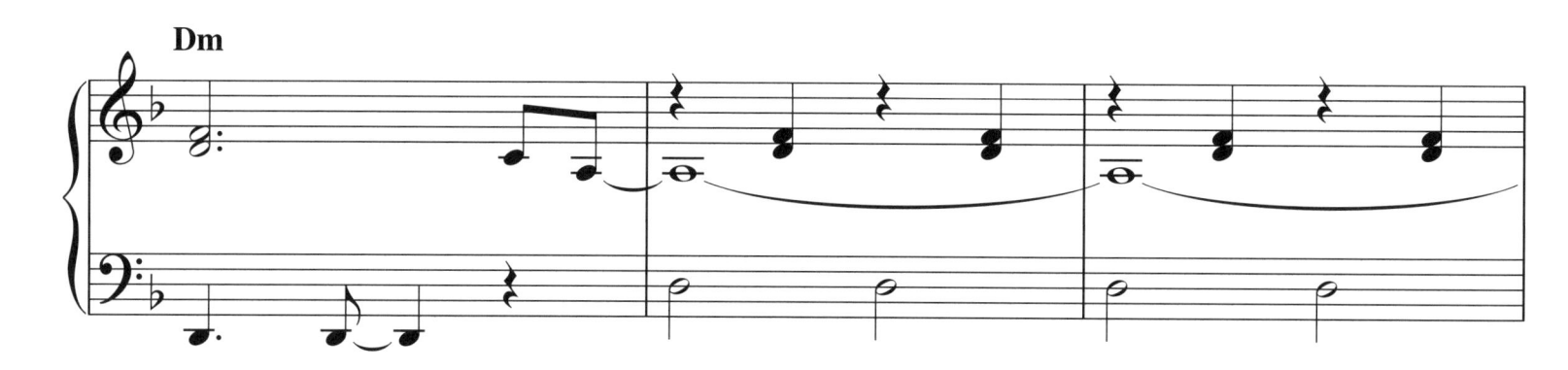

see her, tell her I'm comin'.

She'd bet - ter ru - u - un.

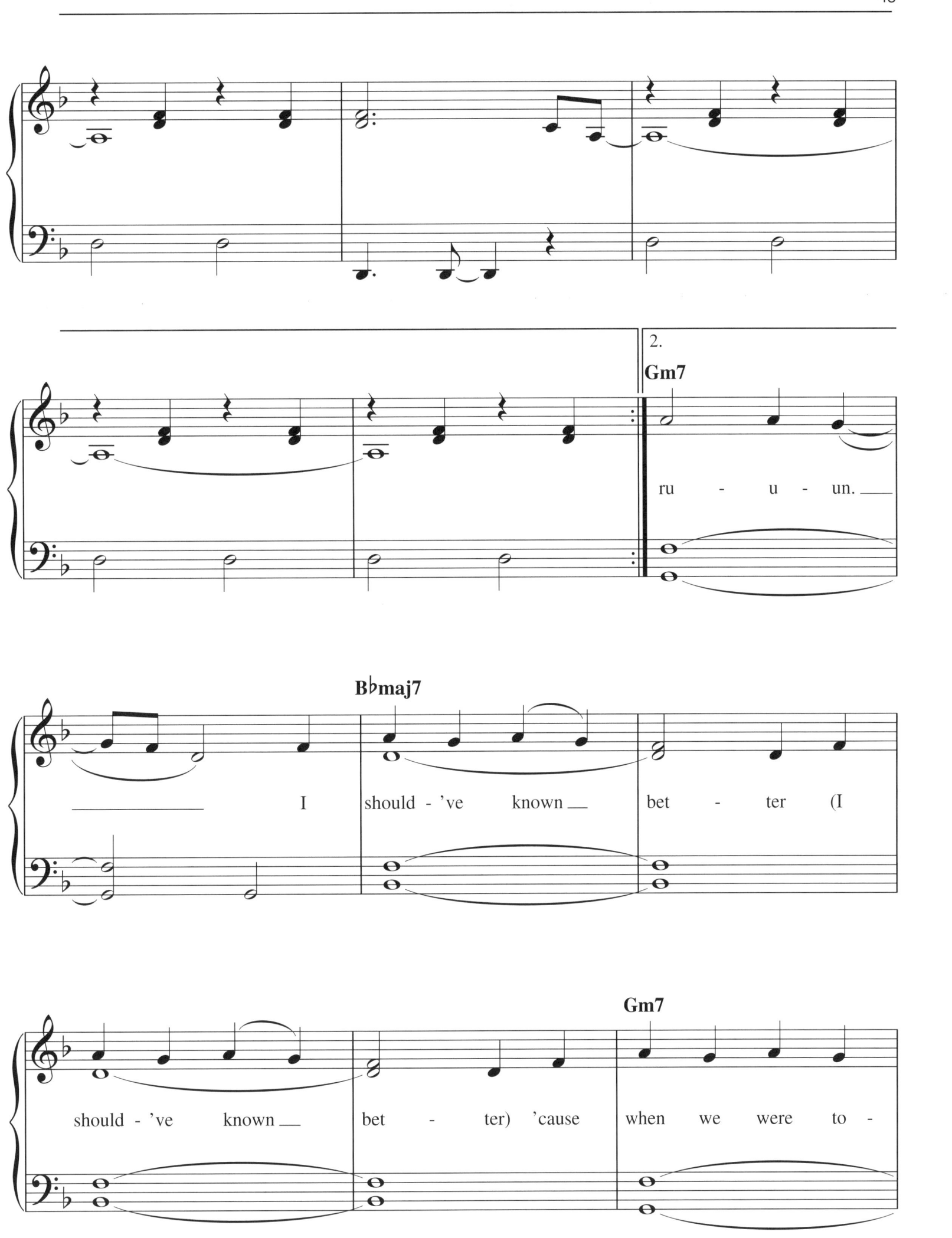

ru - u - un. _____ I should-'ve known ___ bet - ter (I should-'ve known ___ bet - ter) 'cause when we were togeth - er ('cause when we were to - geth - er) she

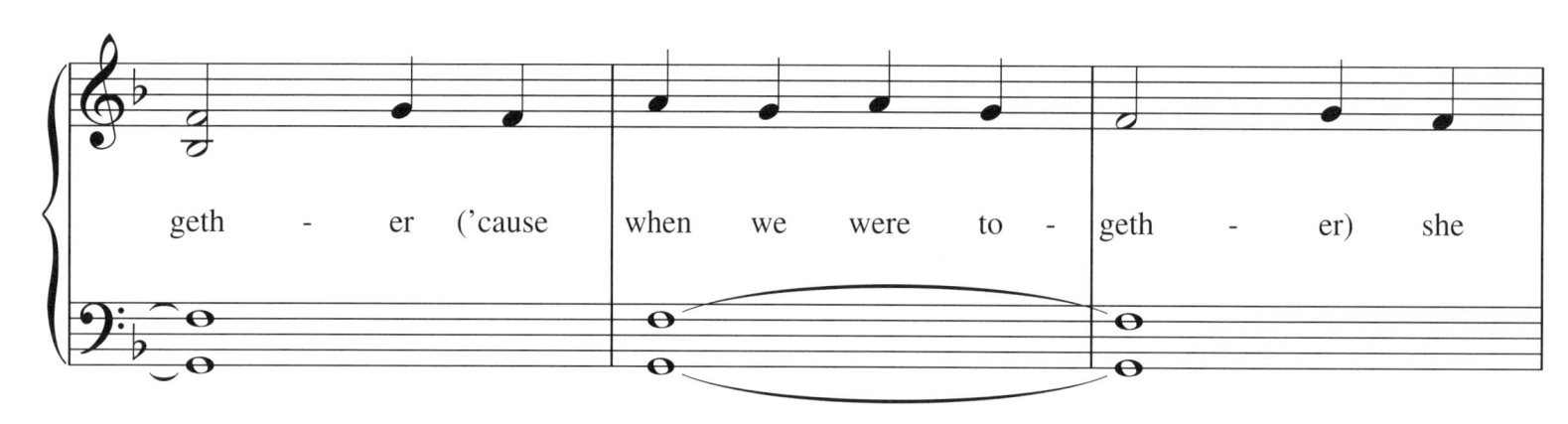

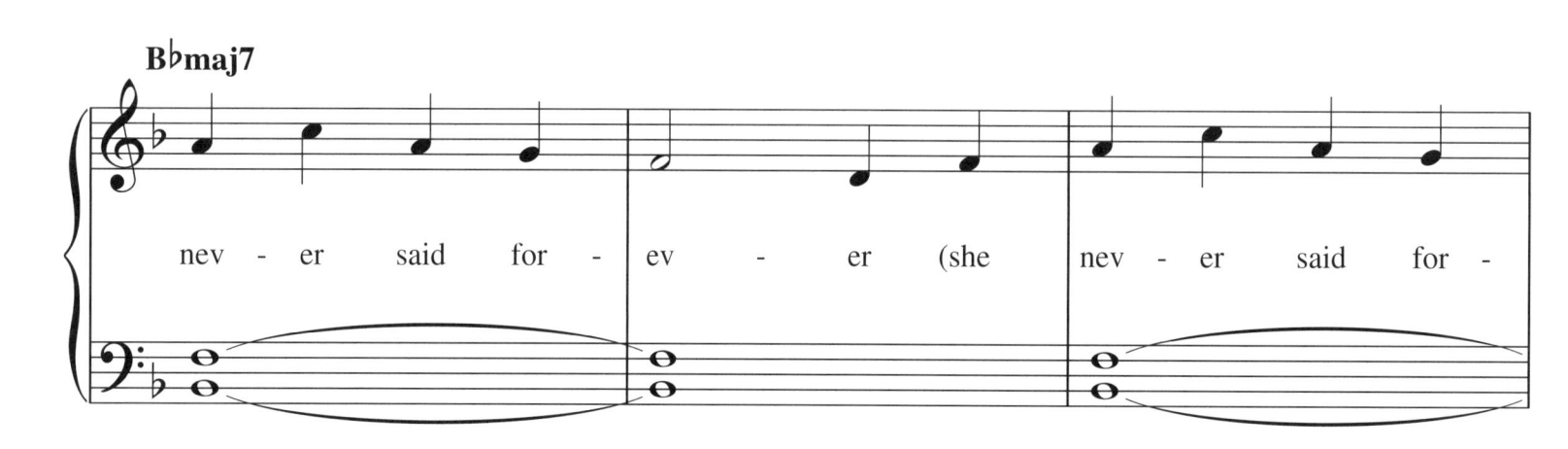

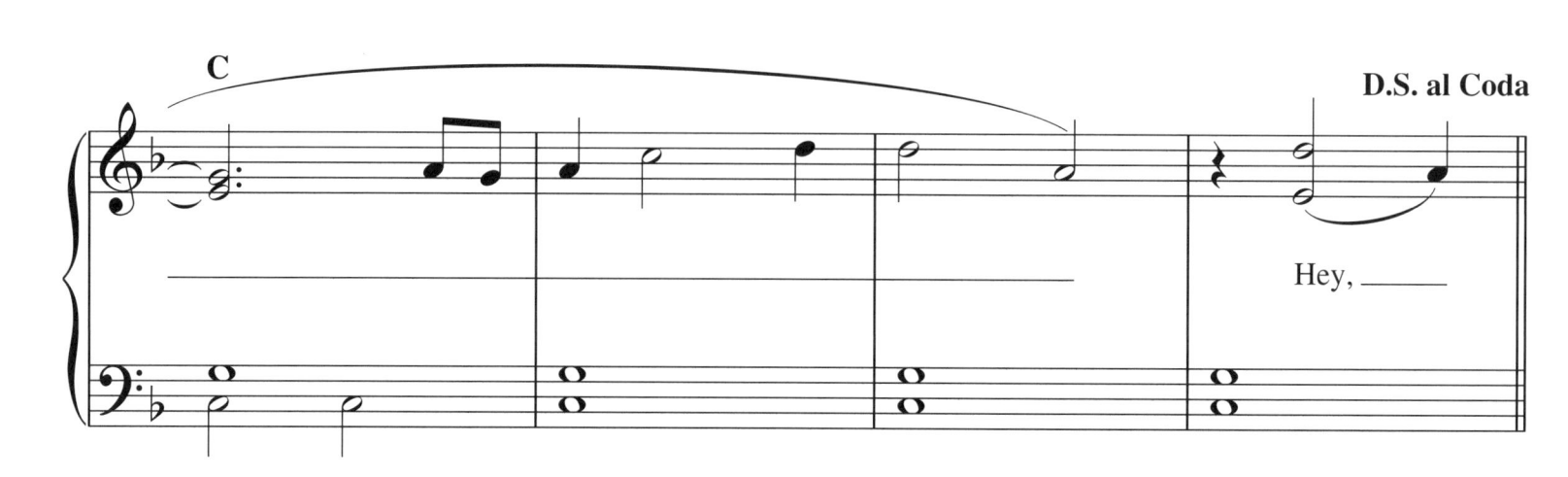

B♭maj7

nev - er said for - ev - er (she nev - er said for -

Bdim

ev - er). I'm the fool that paid in her game.

C   **D.S. al Coda**

Hey,

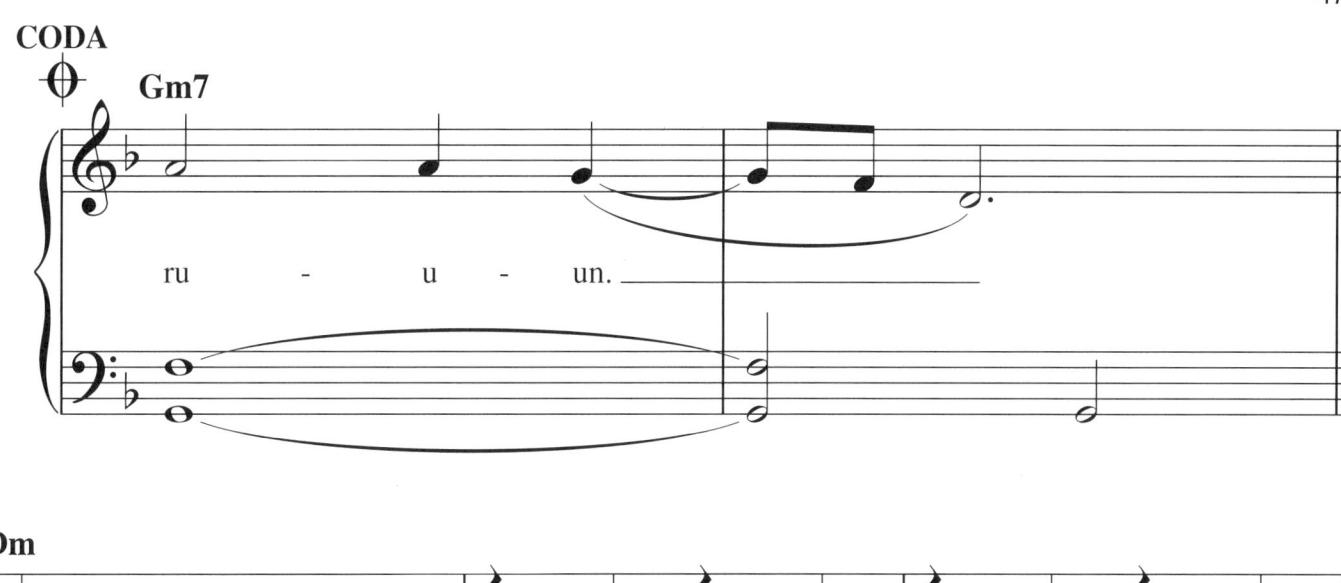

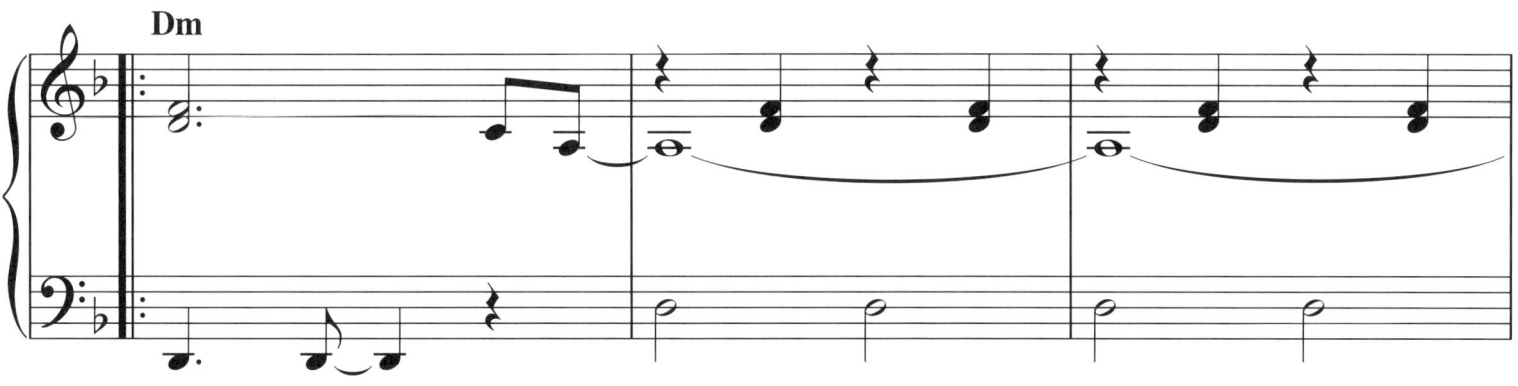

Additional Lyrics

The good Lord better bless your soul,
'Cause I done already cursed your name.
Don't matter which way you go;
Payback's gonna come your way.
You'll be begging me, please, please, please,
And I'm gon' look at you and laugh, laugh, laugh,
While you sit there and cry for me,
And cry for me, and cry for me all night.

I'll spend a lifetime in jail.
(Yeah, that's what I'll do.)
I'll be smiling in my cell.
(Yeah, thinkin' 'bout you.)
Can't nobody save you now,
So there ain't no use in tryin'.
Once I get my hands on you, I'm a ooh!

SHOW ME

Words and Music by BRUNO MARS,
ARI LEVINE, PHILIP LAWRENCE,
DWAYNE "SUPA DUPS" CHIN-QUEE
and MITCHUM CHIN

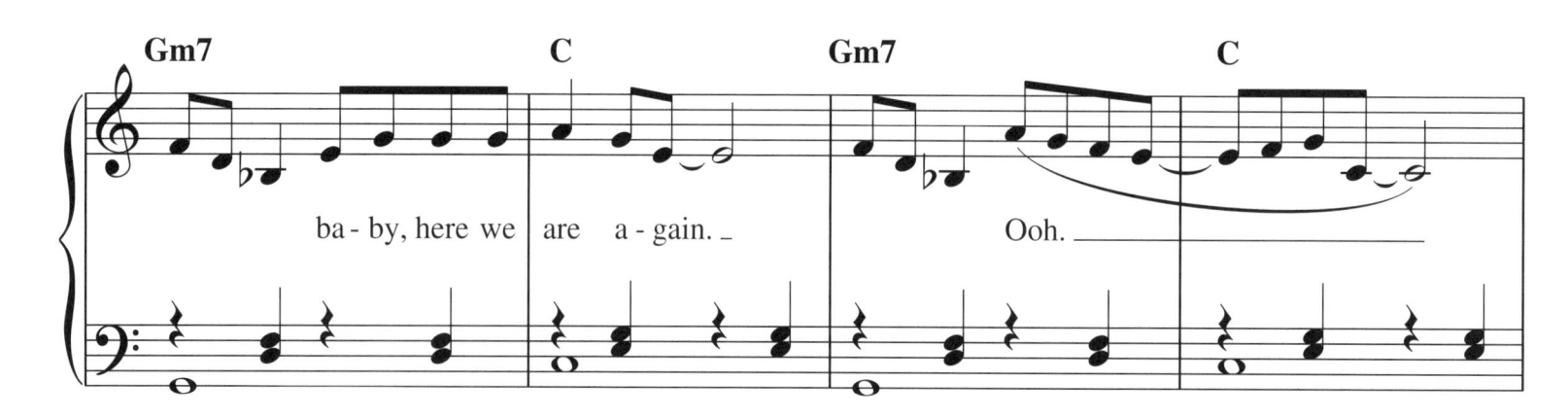

Moderately slow Reggae, in 2

Oh, yeah, oh, yeah, ba-by, here we are a-gain. Ooh.

I can see it in your eyes, you want a good time, you wan-na put your

© 2012 BMG GOLD SONGS, MARS FORCE MUSIC, UNIVERSAL MUSIC CORP., TOY PLANE MUSIC, NORTHSIDE INDEPENDENT MUSIC PUBLISHING LLC,
THOU ART THE HUNGER, WB MUSIC CORP., ROC NATION MUSIC, MUSIC FAMAMANEM, SONY/ATV MUSIC PUBLISHING LLC,
BLACK CHINEY MUSIC, INC., EMI MUSIC PUBLISHING LTD. and NYAN KING MUSIC INC.
All Rights for BMG GOLD SONGS and MARS FORCE MUSIC Administered by BMG RIGHTS MANAGEMENT (US) LLC
All Rights for TOY PLANE MUSIC Controlled and Administered by UNIVERSAL MUSIC CORP.
All Rights for THOU ART THE HUNGER Administered by NORTHSIDE INDEPENDENT MUSIC PUBLISHING LLC
All Rights for ROC NATION MUSIC and MUSIC FAMAMANEM Administered by WB MUSIC CORP.
All Rights for SONY/ATV MUSIC PUBLISHING LLC and BLACK CHINEY MUSIC, INC. Administered by SONY/ATV MUSIC PUBLISHING LLC, 8 Music Square West, Nashville, TN 37203
All Rights for EMI MUSIC PUBLISHING LTD. and NYAN KING MUSIC INC. in the U.S. and Canada Controlled and Administered by EMI APRIL MUSIC INC.
All Rights Reserved   Used by Permission

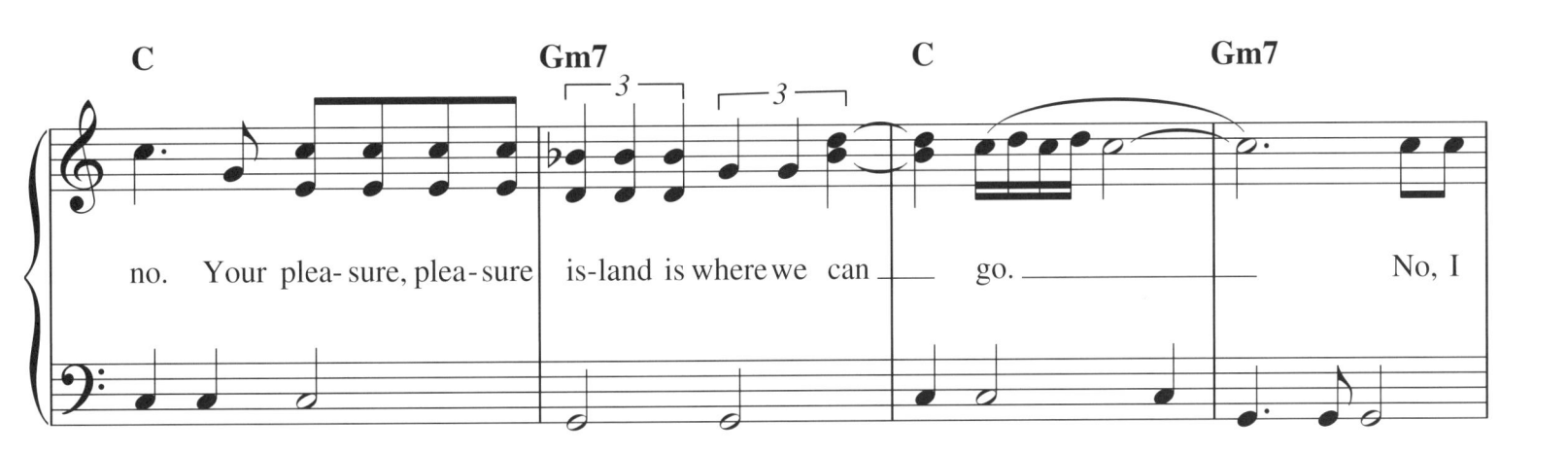

body on mine. Al-right, but don't change your mind, don't you change it, oh, no. Oh, yeah, you called me to-day, drove all this way, so don't let this buzz go to waste, oh, no. Your plea-sure, plea-sure is-land is where we can go. No, I

C
Gm7
C
won't think you're eas - y, no I
won't think you're fast. Your
eyes say, "I'm bus- y," but your
Gm7
C
Gm7
lips get to ask.
No need to fight it when you
know it feels right. You
N.C.
C
say you're a wom - an who
knows what she likes. Then
show me.
Gm7
C
Gm7
C
To Coda
You got to, you got to
show me. You
tell me all day that you're
lone - ly; well

show me, show me, show me to - night. _____ Well,

Love, the way that you laugh, the way that you smile, makes me feel

like you've been wait-ing a while. Well, guess what dar-ling, I've been wait -

ing too. _____ So let's ride; _____ we can get freak-y to -

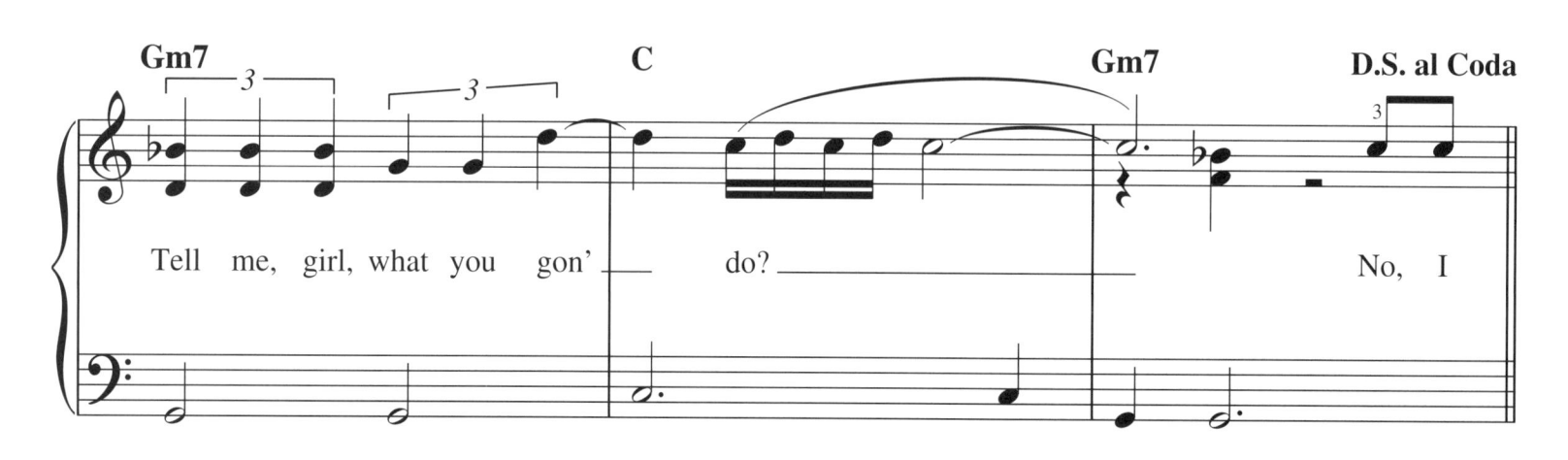

night; right here's your tick-et to ride. Tell me, girl, what you gon' do? No, I show me, show me, show me to-night. It's get-tin' freak-y in this room, room, room. Now let me hear you say you want to boom, boom, boom. We can take it slow, we can

C Gm7 C Gm7
zoom, zoom, zoom. Ba - by if you're read - y for that ah, ah, ah. It's get - tin' freak - y in this
C B♭ C
room, room, room. Now let me hear you say you want to boom, boom, boom.
B♭ C B♭
We can take it slow, we can zoom, zoom, zoom. Ba - by if you're read - y for that
C N.C. C Gm7
ah, ah, ah. Then show me. You got to, you got to

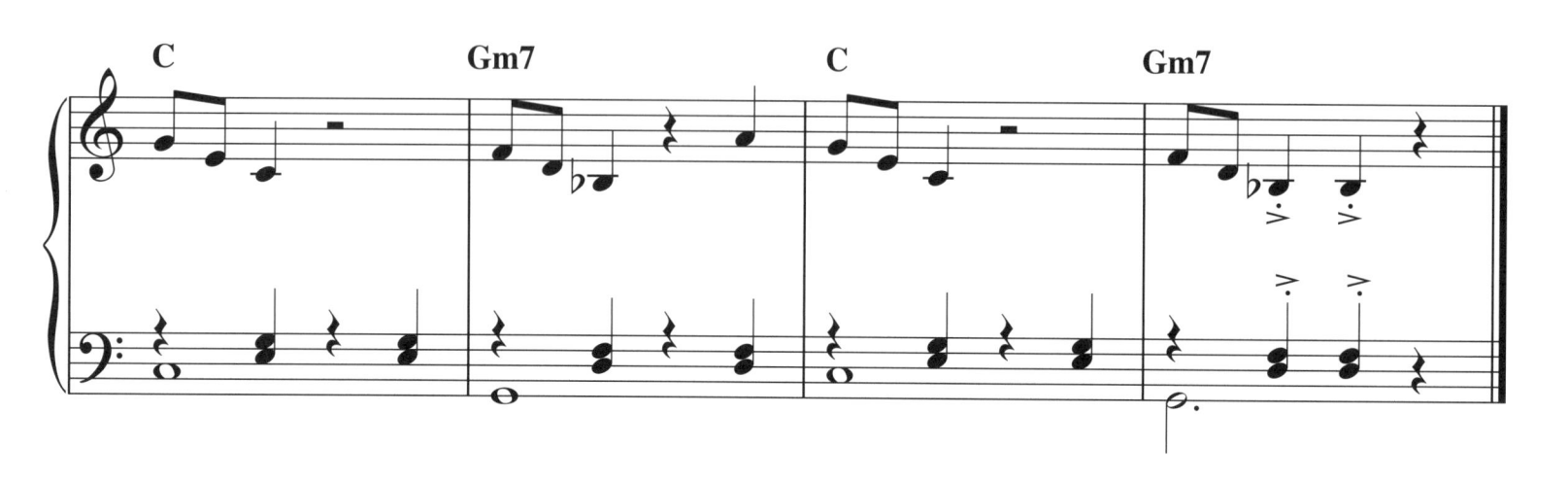

show me. You tell me all day that you're lone - ly; well show me, show me, show me to - night. Well,

MONEY MAKE HER SMILE

Words and Music by BRUNO MARS,
ARI LEVINE, PHILIP LAWRENCE
and CHRISTOPHER BROWN

Da-dat, da-dat, da-dat, da-dat. Hey.

Hey.

Oh, it's not com-pli-cat-ed, so it

won't take a while. You see, mu-sic makes her dance, and mon-ey, mon-ey, mon-ey makes her

smile. (Give her what you got, give her, give her what you got.)

Bm/E

(Give her what you got, give her, give her what you got.)

C#dim/E   **C/E**

(Give her what you got, give her, give her what you got.) Mon-ey, mon-ey, mon-ey make her

Em

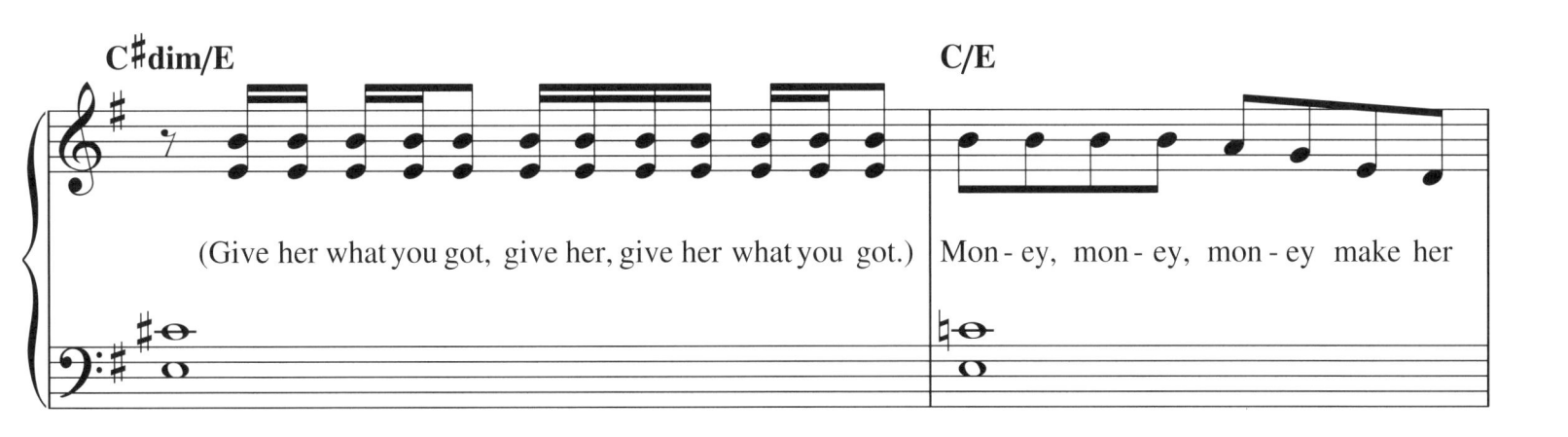

smile. (Give her what you got, give her, give her what you got.)

Bm/E

(Give her what you got, give her, give her what you got.)

C♯dim/E
(Give her what you got, give her, give her what you got.)
C/E
1.
Em
2.
Em
Mon-ey, mon-ey, mon-ey make her smile.
She's a
smile.
Yeah.
Yeah.
Yeah.
Watch her.
(Give her what you got, give her, give her what you got,
got, got, got, got.)

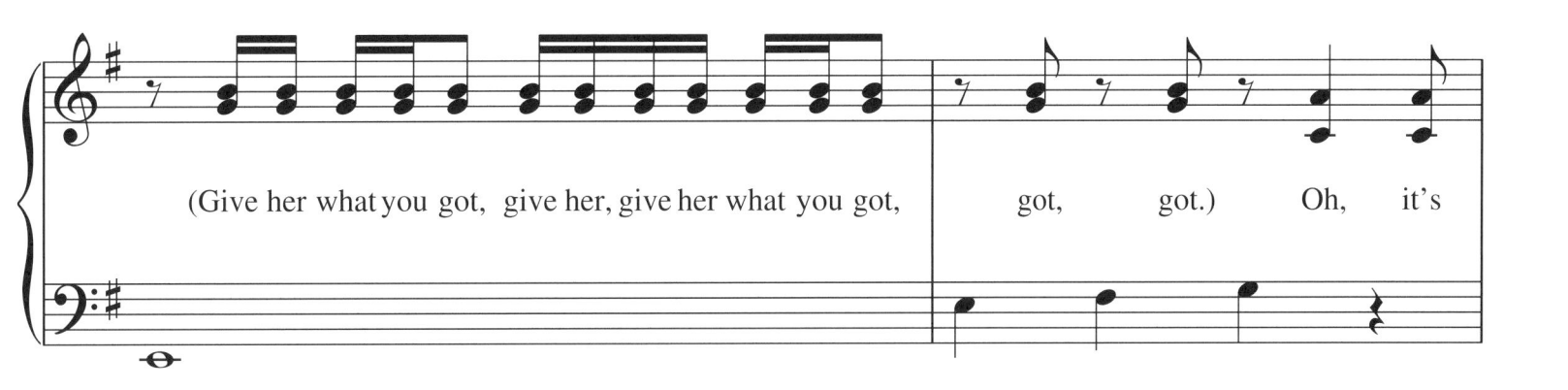

(Give her what you got, give her, give her what you got, got, got.) Oh, it's

G/D not com-pli-cat-ed, so it won't take a while. You see, **A/E** mu-sic makes her dance, and

B mon-ey, mon-ey, mon-ey makes her **Em** smile. (Give her what you got, give her, give her what you got.)

Bm/E (Give her what you got, give her, give her what you got.)

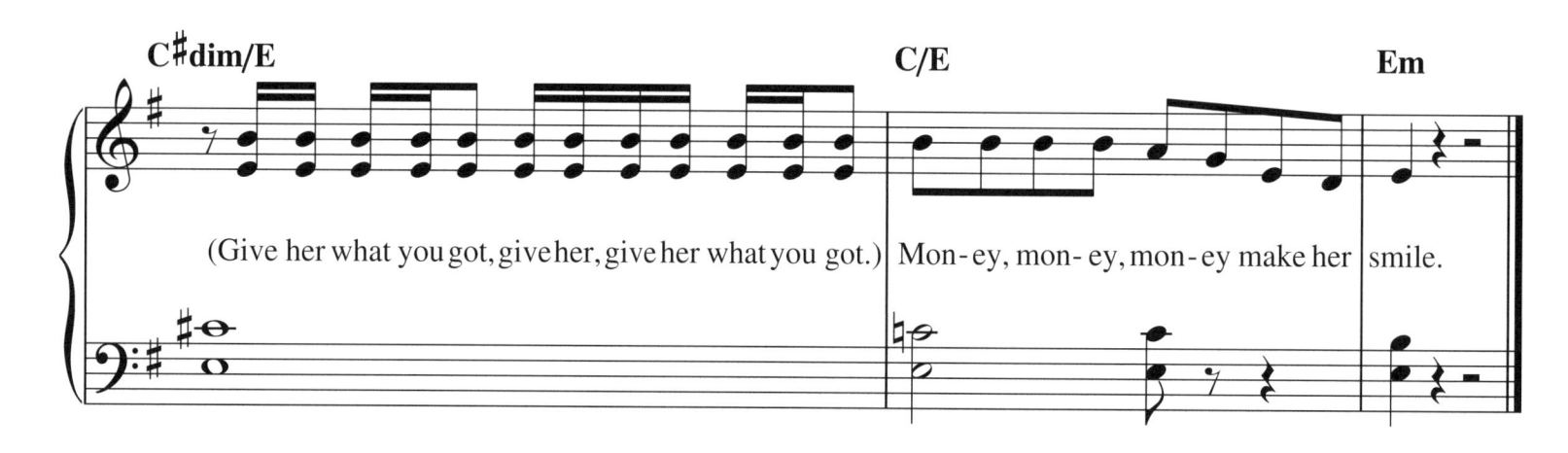

IF I KNEW

Words and Music by BRUNO MARS,
ARI LEVINE and PHILIP LAWRENCE

Moderately slow, in 2

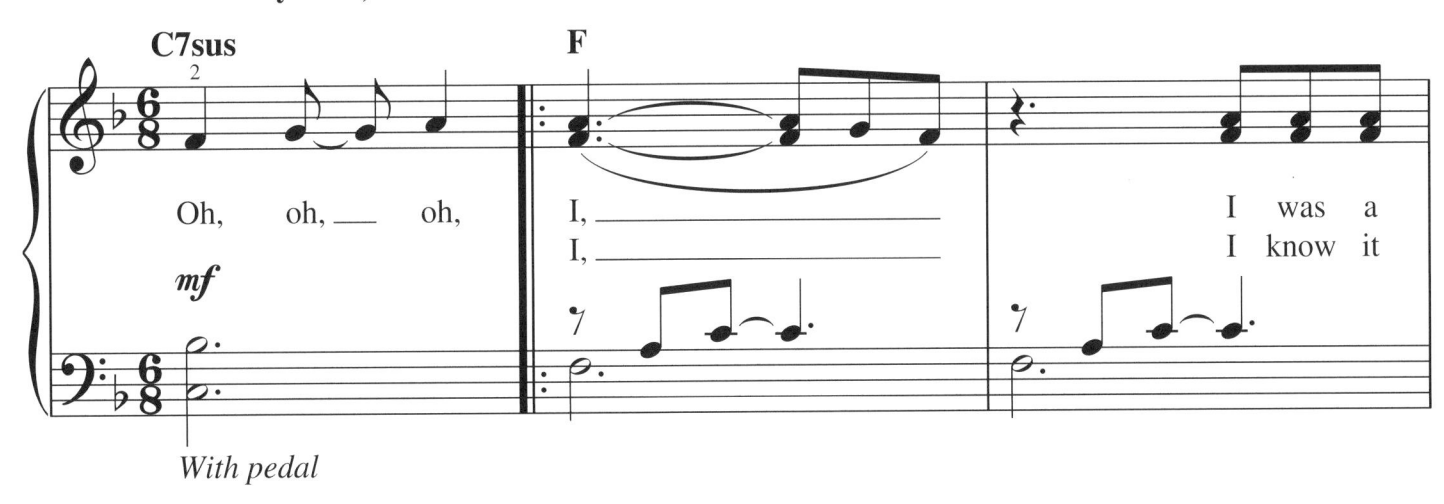

With pedal

Oh, oh, oh, I, I, I was a
city boy; I know it breaks your heart
ride in-to to pic-ture the dan-gers where I'd on-ly one you
al-ways run, a boy who had his fun.
want and love in some-one else-'s arms.
Oh, I would-n't have

© 2012 BMG GOLD SONGS, MARS FORCE MUSIC, UNIVERSAL MUSIC CORP., TOY PLANE MUSIC,
NORTHSIDE INDEPENDENT MUSIC PUBLISHING LLC,
THOU ART THE HUNGER, WB MUSIC CORP., ROC NATION MUSIC and MUSIC FAMAMANEM
All Rights for BMG GOLD SONGS and MARS FORCE MUSIC Administered by BMG RIGHTS MANAGEMENT (US) LLC
All Rights for TOY PLANE MUSIC Controlled and Administered by UNIVERSAL MUSIC CORP.
All Rights for THOU ART THE HUNGER Administered by NORTHSIDE INDEPENDENT MUSIC PUBLISHING LLC
All Rights for ROC NATION MUSIC and MUSIC FAMAMANEM Administered by WB MUSIC CORP.
All Rights Reserved   Used by Permission

F/C
Dm7
Gm
done all the things that I have done ___ if I
C
F
B♭
B♭m
knew ___ one ___ day you'd come. ___ No, ba - by (no, ba - by),
F
1.
C7sus
2.
F7
no ba - by (no, ba - by). Oh, oh, ___ oh, Oh, ba - by,
A
Dm
please, ___ let's leave the past be - hind us, be -

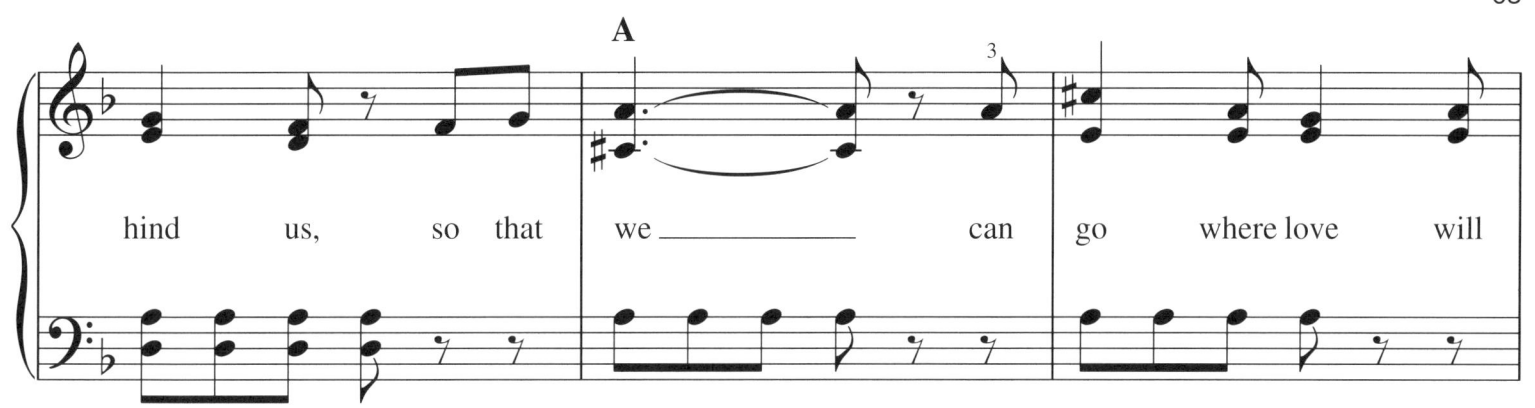

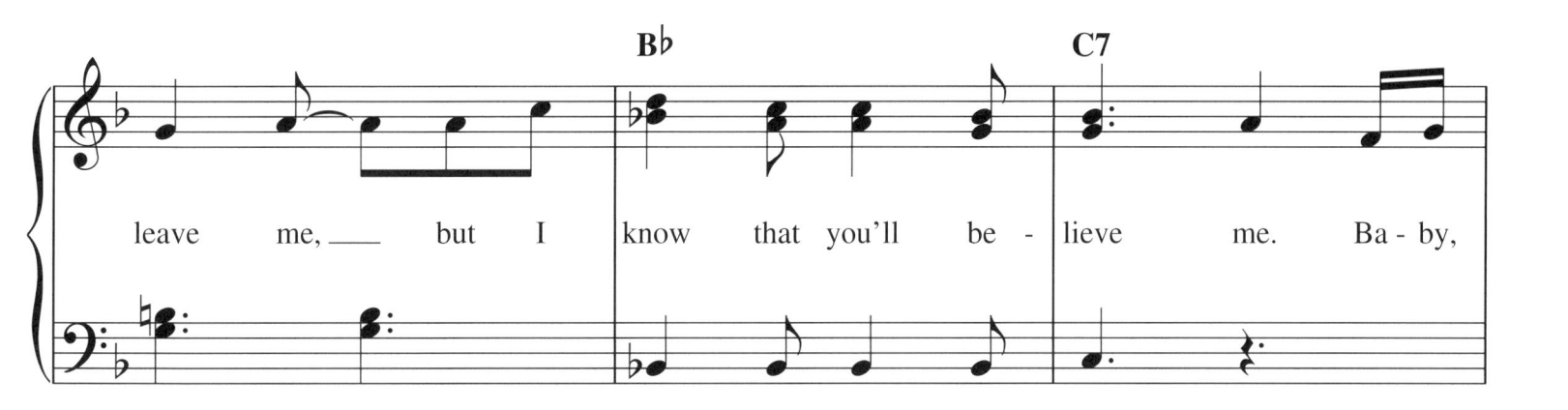

hind us, so that we _____ can go where love will find us, ___ yeah, will find us. ___ I know monsters will leave me, ___ but I know that you'll believe me. Baby, I, _____ I wish we were sev-en-teen ___

Bb/D
so I could give you all the in - no - cence
Bb/Db
F/C
that you give to me. Oh, I would-n't have done all
Dm7
Gm
C
the things that I've done if I knew one
F
Bb
Bbm
F
day you'd come, if I knew one day you'd come.
rit.